W9-CHS-328

TOWARDS MANAGING DIVERSITY
Cultural Aspect of Business Environment

TOWARDS MANAGING DIVERSITY
Cultural Aspects of Business Environment

Deepak Dogra, *Ph.D.*

Foreword By
Dr. Armin Bruck
CEO, Siemens India

4831/24, Ansari Road, Darya Ganj,
New Delhi-110002
Tel. : 23260807, 41563444
Fax : 011-41563334
E-mail: info@essessreference.com
www.essessreference.com

Reference Press
4831/24, Ansari Road,
Darya Ganj,
New Delhi-110 002.

Tel.: 23260807, 41563444
Fax: 41563334
E-mail: info@essessreference.com
www.essessreference.com

Rs.450/-

First Published - 2009

ISBN: 978-81-8405-047-9

Published By Reference Press and printed at Salasar Imaging Systems

PRINTED IN INDIA

Contents

Foreword

In a business world that's becoming increasingly global on the one side and fostering fierce competition from emerging local players on the other, there is a need to define new breakthrough concepts that can complement the established tools of permanent improvement – in order to create a sustainable and competitive advantage for multinational companies (MNC). In this regard, one concept that has recently evolved is Diversity Management. It adds value to the 'being global and acting local' strategy of many MNCs, and offers a promising answer in that direction. However, an in-depth understanding of the incredible 'Power of Diversity' in business is yet to be established for organizations to fully leverage the concept's potential. While reading though Prof. Dogra's book "Towards Managing Diversity", I was enlightened by the clarity of the logic presented as well as the in-depth understanding that it offers for the need to adopt diversity as an approach in business management. "Managing diversity also involves leveraging and using the cultural differences in people's skills, ideas and creativity to contribute towards a common goal and doing it in a way that gives the organization a competitive edge", is a wonderful and illuminating way to describe the needs and opportunities of a diversity approach in Business Management. I am quite thankful to Prof. Dogra for giving me an early insight to his book on diversity, which will certainly enrich the way we manage business.

Dr. Armin Bruck
CEO, Siemens India

Preview

Diversity among employees in work organisations is no longer a casual or chance occurrence. It is actively promoted by many organisations in the west. Professor Dogra has done well to provide a survey of literature and practices now prevailing in organisations in USA and India. He has rightly emphasized that diversity for it to be a source of improving performance has to be consciously managed.

This is so because people do not set aside their cultural values, life style preferences, specially their identities in working life. The richness of cultural experiences could wisely be used with advantage in work life. India has the most diverse population which is also reflected in work organisations, but we have managed it by containing diversity, not for enhancing decision making processes. The book identifies that many organisations in the west have developed practices to improve their performance and strategy formulation. The book is extremely useful for managers and teachers to reflect on the successful ways employed by organisation to manage diversity.

Ishwar Dayal
Founding Director,
Indian Institute of Management
Lucknow

Preface

Thought of writing this book originated while I was working in Siemens, a German Fortune 500 company where guiding policy on Diversity Management clearly stated that diversity was a business imperative and it improves competitiveness by enlarging the potential for ideas and innovation. Policy also stated that when diverse teams address the problems from varied perspectives it becomes more productive and achieve better solutions. Various principles of managing diversity listed in this policy include as follows:

That, we operate in countries with a variety of social structures some are quite homogeneous, others very diverse. Regardless of this variety we promote diversity in all our locations worldwide. The cultural differences of employees with diverse backgrounds and nationalities will enrich our organization, including our central corporate headquarters and the headquarters of our groups and subsidiaries. Qualification and performance for the respective tasks are the only prerequisites for successful employment.

In countries or metropolitan areas with different races, cultural, religious and ethnic groups, we recruit individuals who represent all dimensions of diversity. We motivate them to perform to their fullest potential by ensuring equal opportunities for personal development and professional growth. For groups within society who have not had equal access to education and training, we will actively support initiatives and partnerships to unlock and develop their talent and potential.

We maintain and improve employability by training and continuing education. This applies to all employees irrespective of backgrounds.

We identify high potentials from all backgrounds within our organization and we also attract from external sources, thus maintaining a broad selection for all management functions.

We strive to integrate women at all levels, including top management.

Our working environment will be open and inclusive. We foster awareness of and sensitivity for diversity. The organization will be responsive to the diverse expectations of employees, including work-life balance. We will not tolerate discrimination or harassment of any kind. If there is discrimination of individuals or groups in society, it must not be perpetuated in our facilities.

We promote the employment of people with disabilities and support them to perform their work and to develop their potential. We integrate them into everyday working processes and teams.

It is also essential for us that these principles be applied accordingly in our relations with customers, *suppliers, contractors, shareholders and other stakeholders.*

Since practice have always been a concern for a researcher and not too late when I was reading an article on 'Diversity Management in German and Indian Manufacturing Companies' by Haridass Paelmke & Ronel Erwee, wherein authors have explored German and Indian managers' differences in perception of the diversity management practices in their companies. It showed no significant differences and findings also highlighted that diversity is not viewed as problematic, although the managers' perceptions regarding diversity climate and diversity management competences diverge to a large extent. This led to exploration this topical area of research. This book draws the inferences of western experiences in managing diversity by the organizations through extensive review of literature and some of the data referred in this book pertains to the Diversity Practicing organizations in the west and that of their Strategic Business Units (SBUs) in India.

It is clear that in most of the western countries the diversity not only includes gender, race, ethnicity, national origin, and religion, but also includes disability, age, marital status, immigration status, and sexual orientation. But in case of India, the main diversity categories are gender, religion, ethno-linguistic region and whether individuals belong to one of the traditionally dominant 'Forward Castes,' or one of the traditionally excluded 'Scheduled Castes' or 'Scheduled Tribes,' or the large 'Other Backward Castes' grouping. Issue is not that of

Indian Private sector refraining so far from implementing any diversity management related initiatives but need for the management of Indian private sector organizations to understand diversity related cultural imperatives in right perspective. I hope justice has been done by writing chapters on the Cultural Aspects, Affirmative Action, Equal Employment Opportunity, diversity related HR Interventions, Best Practices as well as on the Indian Perspective of Managing the Diversity. It may be mentioned that two articles on Individual and Group behaviour have been specifically added from my earlier published book for across-the-board reading.

My whole heartedly gratitude for Dr. Armin Bruck CEO of Siemens India for writing such an expressive foreword as well as his siemens like prompt reply to my request even though when he was traveling on a business trip. I can not agree with him more than when he writes that managing diversity not only adds value to the 'being global and acting local' strategy of many MNCs but, an in-depth understanding of the incredible 'Power of Diversity' in business is yet to be established for organizations to fully leverage the concept's potential.

I will be failing in my duty not letting know about Prof. Ishwar Dayal's encouragement as well as a constant reminder that no management consultant or professor can deliver without diagnostic application of management research. His preview amplifies such a need for the cultural aspects of Diversity Management in ample words.

I am thankful to Mr. Sumit Sethi for brining out this book in a record time frame and I am also thankful to Abhijit, Parvinder, Prasad and Yugansh for their help.

Deepak Dogra, Ph. D

www.drdeepakdogra.com

1

Introduction

In this book, use of some terms such as diversity, socio-cultural diverse organizations, diverse organizations, cultural diversity, etc. are used interchangeably. You will read in the following chapter that the literature reviewed demonstrates that organizations with a diverse workforce can provide superior services because they can better understand customers' needs. At the same time since, all the segments of society have a stake in the development and prosperity of society as a whole, creating and managing a diverse workforce should be seen as a social and moral imperative.

INDIAN OR HINDU AND CASTE OR CLASS

According to Indian organizations, a diverse socio-cultural organization meant employees' having diverse demographic backgrounds including cultural factors such as religion, gender, age, demographic background, caste, rural as well as urban background or regional background. It was observed that religion in particular plays a significant part, and by religion, I mean set of organized beliefs that binds people in a close-knit society. However, it should be known that the word Hindu simply means Indian and has no religious connotation. The word Hindu came into use in the sixth century as the Persian rendering of the Indian word *Sindhi* — the Sanskrit name of the river Indus, when the territory around Indus formed part of the Persian empire. Owing to difficulties with orthodox Hinduism, Buddhism rose as a challenge. Hinduism responded by sanctifying the Buddha as an *avatar* of Lord Vishnu, the God of prosperity. Conversions to Islam and Christianity spread in the wake of invasions by Muslim kings and European colonial powers. Caste in India has always been a major source of diversity in Indian society. There are about 3,000 castes in India and each one is a social unit in itself, its structures and strictures differing in each case. So strong is networking that even a change in religion does not alter an individual's position in the caste structure. The nature of the caste system in India is illustrated in the definition of scheduled caste as mentioned in the chapter 3. In India there has also been an endless debate on whether caste is synonymous with class because of the intricate nexus between economic backwardness and social backwardness.

DIVERSITY AND INDIAN ORGANIZATIONS

Almost all organizations refer to diversity in terms of Gender as a prime are of discrimination and surprisingly some organizations have strong discrimination in terms of age. Women are not found in production departments in comparable numbers and the count in finance and HR department has maximum number of women employees. Most of the employees believe that minority, socially disadvantaged, and disabled employees are provided with comparatively less organizational support in terms of working facilities, promotions, and salary increase. Even female employees believe that they have lesser chances of receiving working facilities, promotions, and salary increases as compared to male employees.

Indian managers need to be proactive about learning from diversity and committed in establishing a climate of openness, equity and tolerance. Organizations need to recognize the need for providing training and socialization opportunities that employees are not exposed to in other areas of their lives. It may be pertinent to note that the Constitution of India allows affirmative action through reservations in education and employment and the Constitution also recognizes the principles of legal equality as a basic individual right. The directive principles of State Policy also underscore the Constitution's commitment to social equality. The main challenge the Supreme Court of India has confronted concerned "reconciling formal legal equality as an individual right with substantive equality as a right attached to a group or classes of citizens". So far, such reservations are restricted to government run or government-aided institutions and not the private sector as such. Regardless of whether an organization has a corporate diversity strategy or not, it may be necessary to superimpose a planned change-corporate diversity strategy. At the onset of such an endeavor, corporate diversity, mission statement, vision, and goals must be formulated to articulate the purpose diversity initiatives. This author did not find any single instance where Indian organizations had major thrust on diversity change strategies and it is only at the top leadership this aspect is discussed or if contemplating any diversity leadership development initiatives. Again there is no systematic and planned commitment on the part of organizations to recruit and retain employees with diverse backgrounds and abilities. It is high time that the top management must receive diversity training to address myths, stereotypes and real cultural differences as well as experience of what it is like to be a minority. A diverse workforce also requires efficient communication and leaders must insure that there are open avenues for employees to communicate new ideas, grievances, input and feedback. The classic bureaucratic model is antithetical to the needs of culturally diverse workgroups and innovative, nonhierarchical organizational design may be in order to insure effective communication.

Diversity is an issue and process of appreciating difference within workforce and utilizing this difference and skill base to respond to the needs of the customers. It is using this difference and depth of skills to strengthen the capacity of the organization to respond to issues. It is about getting value for money from the staff, as they are more willing to contribute to activities of the organization if they are valued and recognized. The long-standing involvement in diversity management means a considerable effort for systematic auditing of staff, producing a breakdown by grade and job, on the basis of gender, ethnicity and disability. However, there is no evidence that any organization has conducted any cultural audit. Presence of diverse managers on selection committees and implementing techniques that show diverse people to answer questions to the best of their ability and potential and most of the organizations studied do not have even committees for guiding diversity work.

In order to get a good return on their investment in human capital and maximize their competitive advantage, organizations spend a large sum of their budgets on human resources in the form of salaries, benefits, training development, and recruitment. But when it comes to having a budget allocation most of the organizations have not allocated any specific budget for diversity initiative. When it comes to training, unless training programmes facilitate a real understanding and appreciation of actual differences between people, they are unlikely to have a positive impact in the workplace, training interventions do not successfully tackle negative attitudes towards diversity. Such intervention may again develop unrealistic views about the role that diversity plays within any workplace and leave more problematic diversity issues unmentioned and unmanaged. Therefore, the top management must receive diversity training to address myths, stereotypes and real cultural differences as well as organizational barriers that interface with the full contribution of all employees.

CHALLENGES FOR INDIAN ORGANIZATIONS

The literature on diversity highlights a range of responses to the challenges of diversity management.

Characteristics associated with long-term success of any diversity programs include, but are not limited to, the Corporate Image, Commitment towards Diversity, Corporate Social Responsibility, Effectiveness in Business, Good Business Practice, Legislative Compliances and Ethical Consideration. When subjected testing of questions pertaining to Commitments towards diversity, Corporate Social Responsibility, Good Business Compliance and Ethical Practices, this author found a strong correlation in case of good business practices and legislative compliance indicating that need is for such a legislation. Research has already indicated that the reasons for valuing diversity are:

- to respond to competition, labor shortage, changing demographics and changing workforce values;

- to show that the organization is strategically driven, well-managed and quality-focused to its employees, stockholders, customers, and community;

- to prepare, train and develop company employees to manage and motivate a multi-cultural workforce;

- to gain a competitive edge by identifying, attracting and retaining highly qualified and productive employees and

- to justify itself as a true representative of society.

The manifestation of "care" vary in culturally embedded organizations. The nature of caring behavior and the feeling of being cared are determined by cultural imperatives. Because employees value familial and personalized relationships, like to obey and respect paternalistic superiors, prefer to depend on them for guidance, directions, affection, nurturance, patronage, and so on, the top management should meet these expectations in order to let the subordinates feel that the superior cares. One of the important principles Indian ethos is respect for elders and seniors, and therefore with this commitment elders and seniors are expected to nurture, guide and develop their juniors and subordinate down the line. Most of the Indian workers agree that obedience and respect for authority are the most important things management expects from its employee. The workers in India are equivocal for expressing their liking for a boss who gives clear cut instructions and is more expressive about what happens at office everyday, rather than being controlled by supernatural powers. Workers did not agree that the average performance of all new employees particularly from the gender point of view is as good as others. By adopting and executing the frameworks in this book by systemically managing diversity through a strategically planned change approach, managers will be able to create an organizational environment where they will be able to enjoy innovative, and productive interactions amongst diverse members of the organization.

2

Diversity – A Cultural Aspect of Business Environment

The world has become a much smaller place in the twentieth century as the speeds of communication and transportation increased dramatically. Town and cities have also grown, with their populations spreading out from the center. The early work on scientific management by Taylor in the late 1890s proposed a very mechanistic management style that treated all workers on an equal basis, with motivation based purely on financial incentive. Current thinking suggests that different motivational factors affect different people at varying stages of their careers, and that diverse styles of management contingent upon a particular situation may be more effective. The earliest methods of dealing with a diverse workforce contained a degree of 'ghettoization'. Ghettos have been used since ancient times to confine those minority groups that a society finds useful in terms of skills, but those that culture did not want to absorb. Organizations need to ensure that they do not create actual or virtual ghettos by placing minorities together. The dangers of stereotyping, conscious or unconscious, is all too real, and can create virtual ghettos if all the members of a particular group are funneled into similar jobs.

Modern management theory considers that what a person is showed not be important; if what they can do and contribute to the organization that matters. The successful manager values the contribution that diversity can bring, even if it makes the management task a little harder. A diverse workforce means that more attention needs to be given to the individual and to his or her needs and wants. The pay-off is a workforce in which people feel valued for who they are, and in which people are motivated and thus more productive. Today management has gone from Taylor's ideas of everybody being treated the same, to the current situation in which diversity is welcomed, and people are treated equitably whatever their background or status. Equity is not the same as equity.

If a group of managers had been asked ten years ago to say how important diversity issues were to business performance, most would not have seen the link. Today it has brought a considerable change. Diversity is more of a business issue today, and one key indicator in the number of chief executives who now understand and articulate a business case for diversity. However, those of us who have observed this new environment also feel that the pace of change has been painfully slow.

Historically, theories on Diversity and Diversity Management within the field of Organizational Studies started to develop in 1980s mainly under the influence of managerial reports pointing towards the increasing diversity of future workforce. Today Managing diversity, particularly the cultural aspect of business environments, has taken a global dimension mainly because organizations have become global, so their indigenous staff need to take on board the cultures and the social customs of the areas in which they wish to operate, as well as the cultural issues like hierarchies, gender, the family, social structure and disability etc. The speeds of communication and transportation have also increased dramatically. Town and cities have also grown, with their populations spreading out from the center. Therefore, as mentioned earlier current thinking suggests that different motivational factors affect different people at varying stages of their careers, and that diverse styles of management contingent upon particular situation may be more effective. Today a successful manager values the contribution that diversity can bring, even if it makes the management task a little harder. Contingency theory also suggest that there is no single best method of managing and each manger should use the techniques best suited to each particular situation and to the people involved, and should recognize that there may be different methods of achieving objectives, depending on the organization, the people and the culture that he or she is working with.

When I asked one of the Director HR of an outsourcing company in Gurgaon, he replied that "... every day in our company or organization we recognize people for their unique talent and skills." He also informed that when someone in the office needs a creative story or an opening joke, they know whom to come to for help. Therefore, differences in skills and talents already exists in the organizations, and in some ways, managers have learned how to take advantage of them. This is just tip of the iceberg of the diversity management we know about. Therefore, beyond computer skills the racial, cultural, ethnical and gender differences at work today can cause trouble if they are not handled sensitively. Among the cultural aspects of environment various trends affecting organizations in recent years is the rapidly changing composition of the workforce, a phenomenon known as workforce diversity. It is not unusual for managers of organizations that are expanding globally to find that they are now managing staff from acquired companies that have developed in a completely different culture. Unless both sides have given careful study and consideration to the different cultural contexts, there is always the danger that misunderstanding will affect the building of a positive relationship. Modern methods of managing cultural diversity seek not so much to impose an alien regime, but to combine the best of the organization with the best of the host, whether the host is an actual country, or just those employees with a different background who have come into the organization.

WHAT IS DIVERSITY

Diversity is an important factor in organizational life as organization worldwide become more diverse in terms of the gender, race, ethnicity, age, national origin and other personal characteristics of their members. Today, the workforce comprises people who are different and share different attitudes, needs, desires, values and work behaviour. Implementing diversity has to be an inclusive process, involving the 'root guards' and those who may never have had a voice in the change management process. Diversity is not only about business, it is about morals, human rights and social justice issues as well. In these days of economic rationalism, I feel it is important to not lose sight of the human rights issues around diversity — and that we are all part of the human race.

Diversity refers to the co-existence of employees from various socio-cultural backgrounds within the company. Diversity refers to the co-existence of employees from various socio-cultural backgrounds within the company and includes cultural factors such as race, gender, age, colour, physical ability, ethnicity, etc. The broader definition of diversity may include age, national origin, religion, disability, sexual orientation, values, ethnic culture, education, language, lifestyle, beliefs, physical appearance and economic status.

Diversity can also be looked as basic dimensions and secondary dimensions by putting it through a dual differentiation. The basic dimensions are the ones — race, ethnicity, gender, physical or cognitive capability — which depict differences which are inborn or have influence on individuals during their life span; these are also the core elements shaping perspectives or self-images of individuals. Secondary dimensions are the characteristics which individuals have possessed throughout their lives; in other words, the qualities acquired later on and usually changeable. These appear less effective compared with basic dimensions and have influence on individuals' self-identity and approach while at the same time presenting how these individuals are perceived by others. Some specifications such as individuals' beliefs, marital status, languages, social-economic status, education level, and business experience add new dimensions both to identify themselves and to be identified by others.

Diversity is also discussed in relation to legal requirements, equal employment opportunity (EEO), and affirmative action. Terms like protected groups, adverse impact, compliance, and lawsuit are also frequently associated with diversity programs. The term "diversity management" originated in North American but has slowly taken hold in other regions and countries of the world and it was stated by Title VII of the Civil Rights Act of 1964 that employers could not discriminate on the bases of sex, race, color, ethnicity, or religion. These characteristics, along with more recent focus on disabilities, age, and sexual orientation, are commonly considered as part of an organization's diversity initiatives. However, similar to academic scholars, practitioners also struggle with different views on defining diversity.

There are many definitions of 'diversity management' and numerous terms are used to describe essentially the same thing. For instance, there are various definitions of 'diversity', 'productive diversity', 'diversity management' and 'workplace diversity'. In a pragmatic sense, the common ground in these definitions includes:

- they acknowledge the reality that people differ in many ways;

- they identify implications for the workplace, or society generally, that arise because of diversity; and

- they suggest or imply strategies to ensure that these issues are addressed, in the interest of the workplace, or society generally.

Strategically management researchers agree that cultural aspect of diversity does add value, and that for companies using a growth strategy, diversity can lead to a competitive advantage. Further to that cultural aspect of diversity has a positive impact for organization in terms of advantages in resource allocation, marketing enhanced creativity, problem solving, and flexibility. Additionally, 'diversity' in the workplace includes more than employees' diverse demographic backgrounds, and takes in differences in culture and intellectual capability. It takes more than demographic or ethnic diversity to result in creativity that leads companies to perform better.[124] Three types of organizational goals contribute to the growth of the diversity movement.

First, traditional efforts towards assimilation center around a goal of social justice, a goal that continuous with the modern diversity movement. Moral, ethical and social responsibility goals guide efforts to improve the conditions of racio-ethnic and gender minorities.

Second, legal obligations require organizations to improve racio-ethnic and gender equality. Affirmative action, a key mechanism in meeting legal obligations, refers to positive efforts necessary to eliminate racial and gender discrimination in education and employment recognize the contributions of affirmative action toward racio-ethnic and gender equality, but also note more frequently its limitations.

Third, there is an increased focus, especially by American businesses, to maintain and increase competitiveness in the global marketplace. Corporations acknowledge cultural diversity is necessary to compete in the multinational business environment. IBM, Exxon, Coca Cola, and Dow Chemical, for example, gain more than half their revenues from overseas markets.

The following are a selection of definitions. There is no critical mass that points to a common definition of diversity, but several themes and some nuances, some of which highlight a focus on cultural diversity; equity and inclusiveness.

"It is about giving everyone a fair go, allowing people to fulfill their potential —the bottom line is respect".

"There is a wide variety of understanding of diversity, from Equal Employment Opportunity (EEO) or Affirmative Action (AA) to diversity as a program, to diversity definitely not as a program but as a process".

"Diversity is a buffer against market change. Embracing diversity reduces risk and enhances safety against market changes".

"Diversity means the recognition and appreciations of the unique attributes, background, culture and perspective of all staff, to be incorporated into the psyche so deeply so as to be part of the company culture, and to provide as large a basis as possible, for the attainment of company goals".

"Diversity is all difference that makes each of a special, unique person and it tends to associate diversity with fairness and doing the right thing."

"Diversity is an issue and process of appreciating difference within a workforce and utilizing this difference and skill base to respond to the needs of the customers. It is using this difference and depth of skills to strengthen the capacity of the organization to respond to issues. It is about getting value for money from staff, as they are more willing to contribute to activities of the organization if they are valued and recognized".

"Diversity enables to see more of the world by tapping into it, i.e. about cross-cultural management".

"Diversity means really valuing, acknowledging the similarities and differences, and capitalizing on them for the benefit of the business, society and the world. If there are differences, this contributes to innovation. The initial conflict arising from differences, if managed well, can contribute to new ways of doing things. Diversity is a continuum that covers all aspects of human difference. If is simply difference between people".

"Diversity is about the qualities of being unique and different at the individual and group level — including gender, culture, functional differences, thinking and work style".

"Diversity is a continuum that covers all aspects of human difference. It is simply difference between people".

"It is about going beyond the compliance framework of EEO/AA policies and procedures. Diversity is about organizational or cultural change".

"Diversity means more than color or people. It is about programs that deal with flexible work practices, part-times; it is about giving managers and organizations a range of options that can be used is their business, i.e. Flexibility".

"Diversity means matching the composition of the workforce to the composition of the client for reasons of efficiency and effectiveness."

"Diversity is about two things. One is the lens through which people see the world resulting from their life experience and secondly, it is the thinking processes that people use — the way they are wired."

"Diversity is about how to get people in sales to work with people in R&D, or finance and how to get administrative staff to be valued as highly as the executives."

All above definitions share following three beliefs, i.e.:

(a) Diversity and differences between people can and should, if managed, effectively, add value to the organization.

(b) Diversity includes virtually all ways in which people differ, not just the more obvious one of gender, ethnicity and disability and

(c) Diversity relates to the issues of organizational culture and the working environment.

When we see it in today's context, the term diversity has many interpretations. It is neither so broad as to mean any difference between people nor so narrow as to be limited to difference of gender and race. Diversity is neither another name of affirmative action, nor a name for non-traditional or "minority group" members of organizations, normaly a synonym for EEO (equal employment opportunity). Diversity is the variation of social and cultural identities among people existing together in a defined employment or market setting and includes more than employees' diverse demographic backgrounds.

With the globalizing economy and the increase in multinational corporations, diversity management no longer refers solely to the heterogeneity of the workforce within one nation but often refers also to the workforce composition across nations. The first type, international diversity management, refers to managing a diverse workforce of citizens or immigrants within a single national organizational context. Although the existence of diversity in the workforce is now widely recognized in organizations throughout the world, it is too often viewed only in terms of legal compliance and human rights protection. In reality the implications of diversity are much more demanding and much more interesting. Therefore, the challenge of managing diversity is to create conditions that minimize its potential to be a performance barrier while maximizing its potential to enhance organizational performance.

3

Need for Managing Diversity in an Organization

Indicators or concepts of diversity are not simple. While it is true to say that an individual is male or female, black or white, old or young and so on, people are often evaluated according to the extent of a particular indicator of diversity. Women can be defined as more (or less) "feminine" than others and men as more (or less) "masculine". Indeed, research shows that not only is there a persistence of diversity based stereotypes in most workplaces that have been studied but also that there are limits to which certain characteristics are perceived to be acceptable. There is much evidence to suggest that people can be evaluated negatively by displaying a level of diversity which is deemed "inappropriate", "extreme" or "inadequate".[181]

Regardless of how diversity is defined, the adjustment that employees will make within an organization depend on the organization's tolerance for ambiguity, the demand for conformity, and the value placed on diversity, cultural fit, and acculturation. Today methods of managing cultural diversity seek not so much to impose an alien regime, but to combine the best of the organization with the best of the host, whether the host is an actual country, or just those employees with a different background who have come into the organization.

Diversity Management practice has been started since the early 1980s by the white people. The companies wanted to move towards the kind of environment where an individual employee could realize his or her potential. They started a program named Valuing Difference and it basically focused on personal and group development, EEO on legal issues, and affirmatives action on systemic change. Theory and research indicate that the presence of diversity in an organization or work can create obstacles to high performance for several reasons. To begin, diversity can reduce the effectiveness of communication and increase conflict among workers. Compared to more homogenous work groups, workers in diverse work groups may also experience lower levels of social attraction and display lower levels of commitment to the group. In addition, diversity-related effects identified as harassment and discrimination can increase an organization's costs. The reality is that increasing diversity is not a choice but a fact of life. Given this inevitability, one important question becomes, how can organizations increase in cultural diversity without suffering significant adverse effects on performance? The other side of the double-edged sword is that managing diversity can well improve the performance of organizations on a variety of criteria like implementing the values of fairness and respect for all people.

Today, the workforce comprises people who are different and share different attitudes, needs, desires, values and work behavior hence, need is to include a process of creating and maintaining an environment that naturally allows all individuals to reach their full potential in pursuit of organizational objectives. Managing diversity in an organization requires building specific skills, creating policies and drafting practices that get the best from every employee. It assumes a coherent environment in organization and aims for effectiveness, productivity and ultimately competitive advantage. Through effective integration of diversity management principles in the key human resource functions of recruitment and selection, training and development, performance appraisal and remuneration, an organization can effectively manage workforce diversity.

One of the most significant problems facing today's diverse workforce is exclusion — both its overt practice, as a matter of formal or informal policy, and the perception by employees that they are not regarded as an integral part of the organization. Though diversity grouping vary from one culture or country to the next, the common factor that seems to transcend national boundaries is the experience of social exclusion, particularly in the workplace. Individuals and groups are implicitly or explicitly excluded from job opportunities like information networks, team membership, human resource investments, and the decision-making process because of their identity group. Inclusion in organizational information networks and in decision-making processes has been linked to better job opportunities and career advancement in the work organization as well as to job satisfaction and well-being. Employee's experience of exclusion, therefore, may play a critical role in explaining the connections between the lack of opportunities for members of diverse groups and their discontent with their roles as employees in an organization. If organizations do not become diversity sensitive and learn to remove barriers to full participation of minorities and women, social and economic tensions between majority and minority identity may only increase within the employing organization.

An effective understanding of the concept of diversity requires a multidimensional approach, which needs to be integrated into relevant training and development initiatives. Given the context dependency of the diversity concept, it is entirely ill-judged for trainers to attempt to develop "off the shelf" training courses or initiatives. Training and development for diversity needs to be carefully crafted within individual contexts. Organizations need to develop training and development programmes that encourage "non-traditional" participants to consider different occupations and particular organizational levels. The possibility that segregation occurs due to individual choice, institutional structures, employer choice and "in-group" protectionism need to be explored and challenged so that more effective work outcomes can emerge along with increasingly inclusive work environments.

In addition of fulfilling organizational values, well-managed diversity can add value to an organization by (a) improving problem solving, (b) increasing creativity and innovation, (c) increasing organizational flexibility, (d) improving the quality of personel through better recruitment and retention, and (e) improving marketing strategies, especially for organizations that sell products or services to end users.

Managing diversity in organizations is absolutely dependent upon the acceptance of some primary objectives to which employees are willing to commit, such as the survival of the firm and means establishing a heterogeneous workforce to perform to its potential in an equitable work environment where no member or group of members has an advantage or disadvantage.[225] Managing diversity includes a process of creating and maintaining an environment that naturally allows all individuals to reach their full potential in pursuit of organizational objectives. Diversity management emphasizes building specific skills, creating policies and drafting practices that get the best from every employee. It assumes a coherent environment in organization and aims for effectiveness, productivity and ultimately competitive advantage. Through the effective integration of diversity management principles in the key human resource functions of recruitment and selection, training and development, performance appraisal and remuneration, an organization can effectively manage workforce diversity. It also includes the systematic and planned commitment on the part of organizations to recruit and retain employees with diverse backgrounds and abilities. It is an activity that is mainly to be found within the HRM training and development domains of organizations.

In general, diversity management programmes fall into two categories — changing organizational systems and employee development. Strategies focusing on changing organizational systems including offering flexible work arrangements (e.g. flextime, flexi place, job sharing, etc); providing a variety of support facilities (e.g. on site child care and elder care); and establishing support polices (e.g. support groups, assigned mentoring programmes, door-to-door transportation). If we go beyond these management processes, today diversity management no longer refers solely to the heterogeneity of the workforce within one nation but often refers also to the workforce composition across nations. The first type, international diversity management, refers to managing a diverse workforce of citizens or immigrants within a single national organizational context.

Although the existence of diversity in the workforce is now widely recognized in organizations throughout the world, it is too often viewed only in terms of legal compliance and human rights protection. In reality the implications of diversity are much more demanding and much more interesting. Increasing diversity presents a double-edged sword; hence the challenge of managing diversity is to create conditions that minimize its potential to be a performance barrier while maximizing its potential to enhance organizational performance. Diversity management contributes significantly to the bottom line. The main ways diversity management produces the diversity dividend are:

— improving the efficiency of HRM functions;

— fostering superior decision-making, problem-solving, creativity, and innovation; key factors in the creation of knowledge companies;

— developing cross-cultural capabilities that facilitate operations in culturally complex environments at home and abroad; and

— Implementing new product/service developments and new sales/marketing strategies for diverse customer bases.

Many companies have responded to the diversity effort by offering diversity training. Findings suggest that less than one-third of the companies offering such training perform long-term evaluation or follow up. There was lack of accountability or incentives for managers to achieve diversity in the work arena. Most training programs lasted one day, at most. While three-quarters of survey participants reported a belief that people leave diversity training programs with a positive attitude about diversity, over 50 per cent of the respondents reported that such programs have little effect on a long-term basis.[180] In addition to training in order to reinforce the desired state of managing diversity at the organizational level, revised recruiting, appraisal, development, and reward systems, as well as an enforceable diversity policy need to be implemented. It is paramount that revised policies, procedures, systems, and planned change-corporate diversity strategy are clearly communicated to all members of the organization to ensure that it can be appropriately recognized, executed, evaluated, and reinforced. To reinforce this cultural reengineering effort, management needs to initiate and actively participate in the refreezing stage, the same as they must genuinely participate at the unfreezing and moving stages.

4

An Overview of Behavior: The Individual

Two propositions are widely shared by many writers on management :
  (a) behavior of individuals is caused, and follows a pattern,
  (b) because of this, behavior is predictable. Having said this, it should be added that the behavior of individuals and groups is complex and any temptation towards easy generalizations about behavior needs to be discouraged. A systematic study of behavior is, however, rewarding and indeed necessary for management.

Notwithstanding the caution and a likely margin of mistakes in general, the proximity of the manager with his colleagues and his subordinates does afford him a fairly high probability for accurately predicting the reactions of people at work. We might as well remember that it is doubtful if he can perform his tasks satisfactorily without developing a fair degree of understanding of the people around him. This chapter presents what is intended to help a manager to develop a fairly systematic understanding of behavior in organizations. The data derived are mainly from studies in social sciences. The perspective here is the manager's and the data are selectively taken to help him in his managerial task and for designing his organization and the administrative system.

EARLY PATTERNS

An infant gradually learns social habits right from his birth. He begins to see the distinction between socially right and wrong behavior and attitudes, and acquires his own characteristic ways of behavior as an adult. All these lessons the child learns through his interactions with others in his family and the people with whom he comes into contact.

The child is influenced by his mother, then both his parents and his immediate relations. Reward and punishment teach him how he should behave with older people, with his contemporaries and with those younger to him, how he must share his possessions and how he should compete with others. Many other things are learnt by him through observation. If he likes his brother or uncle more than others because of small favors they do for him, he unconsciously prefers to become like his brother or uncle and acquires a number of habits of thought and behavior from one or the other. This is called, by social scientists, referent behavior. The liked people become a frame of reference for the child.

The child is influenced by the institutions in his environment, family, religious and social bodies, school, political institutions and other formal agencies that may regulate the various aspects of the community's life. From these institutions he learns the distinction between the rights of the individual and those of the community and perhaps those of the government as well. He learns what his obligations are to these institutions. For example, in the United States he would learn about the role of the community's institutions, the voluntary school systems, local law enforcement agencies, etc. In a village setting in India the child would learn about the great influence of the panchayat or the body that arbiters the community's affairs and determines what modes of conduct on the part of the individual are proper and what are not. He observes that the community has indeed the right to regulate the individual's behavior and that in some respects this right is supreme. In Nigeria and in other traditional societies the tribe or the formal community institution has great influence on the child in terms of social responsibility — what is expected of the individual, how a person has to behave in society, who should be given respect, and what values and attitudes are acceptable in social interaction.

The child observes how his brothers and sisters behave and copies them. Sometimes he is scolded for not behaving as well as his brother and he is punished. If such comparisons are made often, and repeatedly, the individual may sometimes develop a feeling of competition towards the object of comparison, or a sense of being inferior, or feelings of rivalry or some resentment about such persons, or the person who makes the comparison. He learns how elders in the family should be treated. He learns how people in authority should behave and how they should be obeyed; in what respects he is free to act on his own and in what respects he must consult his parents or elders.

In a smaller community, such as the rural, the influence of the family and the community is reinforcing. Each institution portrays complementary attitudes and values because the community has significant influence on the family. In a larger city, the community's influence is more formalized and selective. As the community is spread out in larger cities, the influence is varied and diffused. The work place is completely different from that of the community. Social institutions are separated from the place of work. A differentiation occurs between the individual's responsibility to the community and his responsibility to his employers. The social role and the working role become distinct. The social affairs are handled either by a religious organization or a community institution or within the family. The work issues are handled by the management of the enterprise who applies norms of behavior that are different from those of the community. The disciplinary action for deviant behavior in the community, for example, is handled in traditional ways. The same misconduct is handled differently at the place of work. It is often handled in a completely impersonal way. In the developing countries in primarily rural and traditional societies these dual standards are confusing. The unfamiliar ways of behavior alienate employees and the result is disaffiliation of the employee from the management.

In the newly industrializing countries, there is a marked difference between the prescribed standards of behavior in the organization and in the wider community. Over a long period of time, as these countries develop urban communities, these differences will be minimized, as they have done in the industrialized countries. Until the fusion occurs between the community's social system and that of the work place, management in developing countries will have to be especially conscious of the differences and their implications in the industrial setting.

As the development of the individual is a natural process of interaction with local institutions and people, and much of what he absorbs and retains from childhood to manhood is influenced by it, the culture, tradition and values of the community have a great deal to contribute to his adult expectations, attitudes and sentiments. Culture and tradition are pervasive, ensconced in the deeper aspects of the individual's personality such as his adult attitudes, values, and beliefs and the manager has to be aware of them.

Therefore, an individual is influenced by the family in certain ways and by the community in certain other ways.

He has some things in common with the members of his family. He has certain other things in common with members of the community. There are, however, some attitudes and behavior that are unique to the individual himself. How does he acquire them?

Each child reacts to parents and to other people according to his own predispositions which are based on his inner feelings and anxieties. For instance, a child who is extremely dependent upon his mother will interpret her admonitions as rejection and develop a sense of competition with other children. His interpretation of the mother's behavior and his particular reaction to her admonition is colored by his own needs. His very own interpretation and the meaning he would attach to his social interactions will generally bring about differences in his perception of relationships.

Behavior may be modified as individuals interact with new people all through their lives. But behavior modifications are generally possible only if the individual is aware of his own particular bias or way of thinking and behaving that needs modification, and he wants to change this behavior. Rarely are people aware of their own behavior since they have acquired their personality predispositions unconsciously. The deeper aspects of attitudes, prejudices, motives, etc. are buried deep down in the personality of the individual. Changing these requires deep awareness and a very serious effort on his part.

As managers are greatly concerned with certain aspects of the individual's personality, it would be useful briefly to discuss some of these. In this chapter, we shall discuss some aspects of the personality of the individual.

ATTITUDES

Attitudes are a frame of reference, a perspective that a child develops in the process of growing up. Gordon

Allport, an eminent psychologist, defines attitudes as a mental and neural state of readiness, organized through experience, exerting a directive of dynamic influence upon the individual's response to all objects and situations with which it is related. The child establishes the reality of things around him and asks questions constantly to find out what everything is and what it means. It is through the asking of questions that the child establishes his frame of reference for the reality around him and gives meaning to what he observes and hears. His attitudes become a frame of reference by constant filtering of the information that parents of other people in his environment give him. The sifting and forming of the attitudes take place without the child's awareness. The frame of reference developed in the early years and the meaning he attaches to objects and people become a part of his personality and in terms of these he reacts to objects and people in his adult interactions. Normally a person just reacts to the external reality without even thinking about why he reacts in that particular manner.

VALUES

A child learns what is good and bad from how others encourage or prevent him from doing certain things. He may also learn from the pleasure of pain he derives from certain things. He attaches certain positive values to those things that give him pleasure and negative values to the things that give him pain.

When the mother wants to correct some social behavior of the child, she may scold him and say that he should not behave like X from a certain group, implying that X's group is an inferior group. Often statements such as the following are heard in most families:

"You are behaving like a chamar." (a socially deprived in India).

"You ought to have been born in X community and not in this house."

"Where have you learnt these words? They are spoken by, Z people, not by us."

"You are mean like Z."

All these statements convey implied inferiority of the 'other' group. When such remarks are repeated often and by several persons in the child's experience and are derogatory to a certain group, what remains in the child's mind is that group is bad. He does not remember the incident and the context of those remarks. The characteristic is dissociated from the incident and stays as a 'value'. The group under reference, therefore, is associated in the mind with something bad, and this abstract characteristic is a value. Rarely does the adult know why he has a low opinion about X group or a high opinion of any other group. Though he may, as an adult, rationalize his opinion, he has no awareness of its causality. The individual may convince himself that the reasons for his opinion lie in his experience of X group or in the stories he has heard about them and so on. But in objective reality he would, if he tried, find that there are many other members of that group who do not fit into the mould that he has set aside for them.

It is not difficult to see that values guide the individual's relationship with other people. They also influence his likes and dislikes and prejudices. In organizations where people from different groups come to work, awareness of values would seem necessary for the manager if he is to deal satisfactorily with human situations.

PERCEPTION & INTERPERSONAL BEHAVIOR

What a person perceives is in some way unique to himself. The observation goes through a kind of filter built into the individual's personality consisting of his attitudes, values, experience, etc. that guide his perception.

In casual parlance we say there are as many opinions as there are people. It is true that reality differs for each one of us since it is colored by each one's background and interpretation of experiences. These are likely to be different for each one of us. If two persons have certain common experiences between them, they might be able to share common areas of understanding. People from the same family, community or school may have common experiences through which they may perceive the reality in similar but not identical ways. The difference would be caused by the uniqueness of each individual.

The concept of perception suggests that the same thing is seen differently by different people and that one's own way of seeing the external world is logical and consistent to oneself. If A wants to understand B, he must see the reality from B's point of view. This would essentially mean that A must try to understand B's attitudes, values and experiences and discern the logic of B's way of perceiving a situation. A's empathy and sensitiveness to B's perceived reality is a necessity to establish a relationship between A and B. This ability is essential for establishing interpersonal communication in organizations. Interpersonal competence is a major requirement of management because it is the skill with cooperative relationships are built.

MOTIVATION

A useful description of motivation by Jones is: .... how behavior gets started, is energized, is sustained, is directed, is stopped and what kind of subjective reaction is present in the organism while all this is going on. The study of motivation is primarily concerned with why people behave as they do. We like, want, or desire what is a source of satisfaction or pleasure. This we are attracted to seek, choose, and enjoy. The origin of our impulses to do this or that, whether called a want, a wish, a desire, are more generally considered as a motive, that which is 'within' an individual rather than 'without', which incites him to action. In fact, the word 'motivate' means 'to provide with a motive, to impel, incite,' so that an individual can direct his behavior towards an identified goal.

A few generalizations about motivation from the above description are:

— Motivation is essentially an inner-directed activity based upon what gives pleasure to the individual, in his own context. In this sense individuals are likely to have different motives to direct their 'individual' behavior. Conceptually, no two persons would have the same motive to act — that is, to behave.

— Behavior of individuals is goal-oriented. It is purposive. The individual would be primarily motivated by what he perceives as his own goal and his activity (behavior) would be directed toward fulfilling his own perceived goal.

As the individual experiences a need, or wants something that he does not have, he would drive himself to achieve that goal by choosing a modality (instrument) that might suit the circumstances of the situation. Once the goal is reached, a new need would arise and the same cycle would be repeated.

For example, if an employee seeks recognition and promotion, and this promotion is dependant on the recommendation of his superior, he would do things that the superior values. If sitting late in office were to catch the superior's attention, he would sit late whether the work justifies it or not. Sitting late in this context is the employee's instrumental behavior (modality). Needs can be studied systematically and, according to Abraham Maslow, they fall into a hierarchy. Maslow has suggested five kinds of needs:

(a) Physiological,

(b) Safety,

(c) Social,

(d) Egoistical and

(e) Self-actualization.

Atkinson[11] suggests that safety needs are basic and do not fall into a hierarchy. Any time the safety need is threatened, the individual's safety need would be paramount notwithstanding the hierarchy.

Hertzberg's[88] Two Factor Theory of motivation suggests that what gives pleasure to an individual is not the opposite of what gives him pain. The two have separate dynamics of their own. Pleasure and pain giving experiences are not opposite to each other. By asking the individuals to recall experiences that gave pleasure and those that gave pain, Herzberg[88] identified factors that motivate individuals and factors that are necessary for people to work. Herzberg[88] called the first set of factors motivators and the second set hygiene factors. The motivators and hygiene factors of Herzberg are the following:

(a) **Motivating Factors** : Achievement, Recognition, Work itself, Responsibility and Advancement

(b) **Hygiene Factors** : Company Policy and Administration, Supervision, Interpersonal Relations, Salary and Working Conditions

Replication studies of Herzberg researches have been conducted in many countries around the world including India. Some of these studies confirm the findings. Others have found that a neat distinction between hygiene and motivating factors does not show up. Herzberg[88] and his followers have done work in many orgnizations and have used their concepts with considerable success.

David McClelland's[142] theory, known as the Theory of Achievement Motivation, focuses on three kinds of needs: need for achievement (n Achievement), need for power (n Power) and need for affiliation (n Affiliation). He has developed programmes of training to help individuals acquire a greater measure of the three needs. McClelland[142] has shown that the three needs change with individuals as they do with nations. He has provided data to show that successful nations have higher achievement and power needs and that a change occurs in the combination of these needs when the nations suffer decline. His experiments and training have been carried out in many countries of the world. He and his colleagues have provided data to support their main thesis that certain kinds of needs are important for material success and that people can be trained to acquire these needs for high achievement.

THE MANAGERIAL IMPLICATIONS

Whatever theory of motivation the manager may favor, there are certain implications that these theories have for administration, some of which are the following:

— Individuals would be motivated to perform organizational tasks if the task goals were congruent with their personal goals, or at least, if they perceived that they would serve their personal goals by being a member of the organization and by performing the organizational tasks.

— The supervisor cannot directly motivate an individual. He can however create conditions in which the individual can discover congruence between his personal goals and the organizational goals.

— The personnel and organizational policies of the administrator would have to consciously include steps for motivating people; at employee is likely to be motivated if the motivating factors are built into the work system.

CONCEPT OF SELF

As a result of his varied interactions with people in the social environment, an individual develops a concept of himself, his abilities, strengths, his contribution to the society and other factors concerning himself. It is his self image. Throughout the period of growing up the child gradually learns from his interactions with other people what he may become when he grows up, what he is good in doing, what his parent's expectations of him are. From varied interactions of this kind, he forms an image of himself, his capabilities, his ambitions and what other people ought to think of him. The image changes as he acquires new experiences, as he interacts with new people and situations. For example, when he goes to a new school and has more severe competition, he may have to modify his self image as the best student in class or the best player on the playing field. At times he sees the new environment as being unfriendly. He develops a sense of being inferior. For example, when he goes to a developed country for higher education and suddenly observes that he is treated differently from others in his class, he either becomes withdrawn or he becomes aggressive or he tends to imitate those who according to his own predisposition are treated better. The individual is rarely consciously aware of his self image or of the reasons why he suddenly dislikes his stay abroad when he has looked forward to it with the greatest degree of hope and pleasure.

Most people have to go through changes in their self image. Sometimes the change occurs through painful experiences. Employees migrating from rural to the industrial environment are likely to experience discomfort in their formal roles and relationships in large organizations.

Instead of the community's natural acceptance of him and his membership which was never questioned unless one committed a major social misdemeanor, the organization's acceptance of him depends only on the condition of obeying the supervisor's code. Instead of an affinitive environment he finds himself in a competitive environment. Instead of being a somebody in his community he is lost in an impersonal structure where he feels like he is a nobody. He has grown in an environment in which personal relationships and mutual acceptance are the basis of life. His image of himself as a respected person to whom other people responded warmly is shaken. In order to preserve his image in his own eyes, he does a number of things: he may blame the manager and the management for lacking human feelings and become a strong supporter of the trade union. He may be absent as often as he can. He may become totally indifferent to his work and put in only the minimum effort. He may become psychologically ill. These are the defenses he employs against the attack on his self image. They are known as defense mechanisms.

The most common of defense mechanisms in the work situation are withdrawal from active involvement in work, aggression against those who have caused the hurt, rationalization by ignoring that anything on his part is wrong, repression of resentment and anger which may be released in unpredictable ways. These symptoms are important enough for a manager to recognize and take appropriate timely action to restore the worker's self image and to get him to cooperate as part of a team.

INDIVIDUAL DIFFERENCES

Certain common patterns as well as unique patterns of behavior develop in the process of growing up. Individuals have their own preferences, their likes and dislikes, their different skills and competences. One may have managing skills, another may prefer a production job, a third may like designing, a fourth may have skills for training others. If the manager is able to determine what an individual recruit's preferences are, and what employees would best fit into what jobs, he is on the way to being a good manager.

Personality differences too have to be noted. One may like to be left alone to work on a job that requires his direct contribution. Such a person may improve his performance if he is allowed to compete with himself by giving him his performance data at regular intervals. Another may like to work with a group and derive great satisfaction in being a member of a certain group at work. There are differences also in the styles of working. One person would produce his best if he works for short intervals with short periods of rest in between. Another may prefer to finish his work in one stretch and take longer leisure time to do something else. Still another may want to do several things together and another may like to do one thing at a time.

The habits, preferences and individual inclinations of a person have a personal history. The fact emerges that he will be able to do well when conditions he considers suitable are provided. Again, some individuals are able to adjust to new situations more easily than others. In all cases, the manager has to be able to know the differences between individuals and facilitate their adjustment to an unfamiliar environment. Disregard of individual differences causes more problems than are suspected in the performance of the enterprise.

As discussed the important forces that play upon the formation of an adult personality, are the forces that influence and guide his behavior as an employee. The subject has been discussed in a general and broad manner and is intended to provide understanding of a 'living' person — how he acts and reacts to situations.

5

An Overview of Behavior: The Group

In every organization groups exist. It is necessary to understand how they are formed and how they function because they have a decisive influence on the behavior of an individual. They can play a significant role in improving or restricting output depending upon the group's perception of the task and of the management. They can be a stabilizing influence in building up cooperation at work or they can be disruptive. Here we will briefly discuss group processes and will later show how groups interact among themselves.

Groups do not form by accident. They are formed where certain conditions exist. A comprehensive definition of groups can be formulated in terms of the following characteristics; (a) interaction between individuals (b) perceptions of mutual membership, (c) the development of effective ties, and (d) the development of interdependence of roles. When people have a shared goal and each member regards others as members, and they are all able to freely interact without social differences among them, they would emerge and function as a group. There is a clear distinction between an aggregate of people and a group. People assembled on the pavement to see a show of some kind may have a common goal, i.e., to see the show, but each person is an individual and there is no mutual perception of membership or interaction among them. A study group or football team is different from the aggregate of individuals in so far as it has a shared goal, mutual membership, interaction among the members and, as a result of these, effective ties and interdependent roles. Not every assembly of people is a group. It must have the required conditions to act like a group.

Systematic studies of groups have shown that they develop a fairly formal structure to govern social relationships. The leader is accepted by most members and regarded as such, a social status and hierarchy among members is established and ways are developed of rewarding and punishing members for enhancing or deviating from the group's interest. In return, the group lends its full support to all its members and gives them protection in whatever respect it might be needed. In industry it has been commonly observed that fast workers spend time helping their slower colleagues even at the cost of the higher wages they might have earned for higher individual output. Slow workers are protected by the group as well as by restricting output so that they do not become targets for pressure on the part of their supervisors. There are instances in almost all societies where the entire group has accepted punishment from the management for not revealing the names of the true culprits in misdemenor or crime from among them. In other instances when groups have been requested to set their own targets of production and are given the freedom to function as a group, they have set higher targets than the management may have done on their own.

The group's strength lies in the mutual interdependence between itself and its members. More successful the group is in achieving its perceived goals, the more cohesive is it likely to be. If it is successful in keeping the production targets low and in defeating all the various measures that the management might take to counter them, the group will have greater solidarity or cohesiveness than it would in the face of defeat. If the social organization of a group is disrupted by its defeat, the members would invariably be disaffiliated and the probability is that it would have factions within itself. If the management wishes a group to be effective and function as a group, it would have to ensure that conditions exist for it to function effectively, including a sense of achievement to make it cohesive.

Group cohesiveness is achieved through mutual satisfaction between the individual and the group. The individual gets recognition, identity, a say in its affairs, satisfaction of at least some of his goals, etc. At the same time, the group as a group is able to work together and it can retain its own identity; in doing so, it can achieve its shared goals. This mutuality is necessary for a group to become cohesive and to be able to successfully influence its members. Many successful supervisors consult the leaders of various groups about the changes that the management might want to introduce in the organization before it draws up its plans of action. These consultations give the supervisor a clear enough idea as to how successful the changes are going to be and how well employees would receive them.

The power of groups on individual behavior is pervasive. What the group members say is automatically believed to be true because there is a mutual trust and understanding among them. The same may not be acceptable to the members if the management were to say it. Severe punishment for deviant behavior is accepted from the group leader and is often resented strongly if it comes from the management. In serious issues the group is known to use coercive methods to discipline its deviant members. At times, some members might disagree with the group action, but most of the members will go along with the discipline of the group leadership in view of the protection and support that member's need from it. A most common example of this phenomenon is the trade union confrontation with management. Many members may disagree with some action or strategy of its leadership but they will conform to its call for action. The differences among its members will only show if the trade union appears to be losing its battle against the management in a prolonged struggle. Under unfavorable conditions the trade union is likely to gradually lose its influence over its members and develop factions. In fact, there are always some factions in large groups such as a trade union. Under conditions of prolonged stress and failure these factions become pronounced. In a small group factions are not very common.

The ties that individuals have with groups differ. The more eager an individual is to become a member of a group, the more he is likely to conform to its norms of behavior. The individual's motive for membership is important. If he becomes a member of the group because he is able to fulfill his need for affiliation or recognition, the more heavily would he lean on the group, even if he has to conform to norms some of which he finds cumbersome. If the motive is to get even with his supervisor for hurting his self image, or some other personal reason, the individual is likely to go a long way to conform to the group's norms. If the individual does not derive a great deal of personal satisfaction from the group, the probability is that he would not wholeheartedly follow all the norms laid down by its leadership.

Management has to work with groups. An understanding of the whys and wherefores of their formation and of the way they function is essential for dealing with them. Briefly, the following characteristics of the groups are important:

— Groups always exist in every organization whether they are recognized by the management or not. If they are not recognized, they can seriously interrupt the working of the company.

— Groups are formed around the common interests of its members. Members believe that the group can give them what they need and, in return, they give the group their support in ways that make it strong. The common goal may be something that may involve the organization or not. It may be high output or low, or leisure time or recreational games or activities, hobbies or just membership of a tribe or a caste. Many employees are members of a number of groups. If there is conflict among the membership of various groups, the individual suffers some emotional strain and will move to reduce or eliminate the strain by resolving the conflict in the direction of the strongest of his group ties.

— As most social groups are based on voluntary association, the members are more willing to conform to the discipline of groups than they do to groups in which membership is imposed by someone else, such as work groups in organizations. Management in many organizations now use this knowledge to encourage the employee to make his own choice of work group in which he desires membership.

— Groups become cohesive when more members conform to its established norms of behavior. In situations of conflict, the group leadership demand greater conformity of its members and, consequently, during periods of conflict, the group is likely to be more cohesive.

— A group is different from an aggregate of people. Its members have shared goals; they perceive others as being members and they are able to interact with them freely.

A group develops its own social structure. It has leaders that most people accept as being capable of achieving the goal that the group may have set. It evolves a code of conduct, a social status for its members and a distinct method of rewarding and punishing the members. Management could use group processes for developing common purpose between itself and the employees, or it could disregard these processes and allow them to become a source of disruption of organizational tasks and relationships.

INTERGROUP BEHAVIOR

Just as groups have a distinct social structure and behavior, they also have a recognizable dynamics in their relationship with other groups. When equally developed social groups have to share resources or work with other groups, they develop mutual feelings of competition and sometimes hostility. If the groups are not equally developed, one group becomes dependent upon another and may resent the other for such dependence. The feelings of mutual hostility show up in their intergroup relationships. Whether they cooperate or come into conflict would depend upon the way they function. The conditions governing each are discussed below.

CONFLICT

If two groups are competing, and each has a separate identity and pride in its own group (cohesiveness), they will have feelings of hostility. The winning group is likely to be a target of hostility on the part of the losing group. The loser will show internal disorganization. The probability is high that the leadership would be under severe strain and would run the risk of changing. The winning group is likely to become even more cohesive than before.

A losing team has a higher probability of change in its leadership and the constitution of its team than the winning team. Often the successful team would find it difficult to change its membership or its constitution. And periodically, for this reason, it may lose its winning strength over time. Hence success also has its negative effects on the team almost as much as defeat has.

It has often been observed that after a long battle with the management, a trade union suffers many changes if it has lost in the struggle. The union is invariably threatened by its dissident members and the leadership is under constant attack irrespective of whether the leaders are able to retain their leadership positions or not. This phenomenon is also observed when major political parties lose highly controversial elections in the country.

Within the organization, struggles are common between staff and line employees, production and sales, planning and finance; between headquarters and branch organizations, etc. The battles in these cases are fought in a variety of ways. Sometimes data are withheld by one from the others, or proposals of one are invariably opposed by the other, or surreptitious 'games' are played that most people in industry recognize. In rare instances the conflict is open. Winning and losing are judged by which group is able to influence the top management most. The consequences of winning and losing are about the same as in the case of the union and management situation above. Leaders lose their influence and their followers decrease. As this happens, other persons gain influence.

Conflict between groups has its own dynamics and both loser and winner have to face certain short and long-term consequences of their losing or winning. In one sense, both groups lose in the long run as was explained above. Research suggests that hostility between groups may not affect relations between individual members of rival groups. Hostility is transferred from group to group. As members of two separate groups, individuals may be friends and may be able to establish mutually satisfactory relationships as individuals. Executives from the competing departments may work well together as members of a newly created task which has nothing whatever to do with their respective departments. When dealing with the department as a group, they might, however, still be hostile. In the same way each competing group may have its own culture cooperation within its own structure. But this culture is unlikely to be transferred to its relationships with other groups.

Communications within the same group is easy. It is free of distrust, hence generally accepted by members. Members are interested in knowing things that concern them as members and would keep their eyes and ears open for information. This characteristic of communication was recorded by the finding of a study of the management of trade unions. The results show that the methods of communication within the union were less elaborate than within the management, and yet they were more effective than the management's. The reason simply was that union members felt a personal involvement in the communication that the union made and sought out information from the union. In groups members are thus involved and communication is much more direct: it is more easily trusted and therefore more effective.

COOPERATION

Intergroup research suggests that groups will cooperative under certain conditions, the most important of these being the sharing of a common goal. Sherif, who has done pioneering work in intergroup conflict and cooperation, calls this the Superordinate Goal. It is so termed because the two groups have to evolve goals that are shared by both: invariably they are not the goals that each of the groups respectively had. Evolving goals that both groups can share is an important condition for cooperation between groups. When groups work jointly toward the common goal, each group will experience abatement of hostility and gradual development of mutual trust and confidence.

Mere contact between groups, each having its own goals, would not reduce intergroup hostility and conflict. For instance, equal treatment meted out by management to two rival unions, or two hostile departments, is not sufficient to reduce hostility and increase cooperation between them.

EFFECT OF IMAGES & STEREOTYPES

Image is the picture one group may associate with members of the other. When A thinks of B, a picture of certain characteristics is conjured up in A's mind. This is A's image of B. Stereotype is a preconceived image of a person or one group by another.

Certain images about the other group facilitate the development of hostility between two groups. Many of these images are formed in childhood and people are not fully aware of the reasons for these images. Stereotypes about people and groups also develop through childhood interactions, and are often justified by the individual by finding evidence in support of his stereotype. These images and stereotypes, however, significantly influence intergroup relations. For instance, many people have certain stereotypes about others: the hard ruthless character of B group or the selfishness of X group or the laziness of people from the less developed countries. While working with these groups the individual's images and stereotypes about them will unconsciously influence his behavior. At times the image is reinforced even when one person from the said group happens to fit it.

Carl Rogers, whose contribution to the understanding of interpersonal relations is significant, makes his point thus: 'Each party may hold: My view is the right and the true one. You are unfortunately mistaken and inaccurate in your view of the situation and in your analysis of what it means. Your view is false and wrong, yet you stubbornly hold to it'. Rogers also suggests that in tense situations there is also a value judgment, saying: 'I am honest and straightforward and fundamentally good in my approach to our relationship and its problems. Unfortunately, you are none of these things. You are essentially bad and evil and untrustworthy in your approach to the whole situation. My motives are good, yours are not'.

Images, stereotypes and personal values account for causing interpersonal and intergroup conflict. From the point of view of the manager, some of the most important aspects of intergroup relations are the following:

— Conflict and harmony each have their own dynamics. They develop in certain ways that lend themselves to the systematic study of each. Conflict is not the opposite of cooperation. Absence of conflict does not necessarily mean presence of cooperation. Each has its own logic and management has to make efforts as much to remove conflict as to develop cooperation.

— In conflict, groups have to face consequences of both winning and losing. Winning reinforces the structure of the group and tends to freeze it. Consequently, change in structure becomes difficult. The losing group invariably develops factions and its leadership is put under serious stress and often displaced.

6

Affirmative Action and Equal Opportunity : A Paradigm

Many a times Diversity is discussed in relation to legal requirements, Equal Employment Opportunity (EEO), and affirmative action. Terms like protected groups, adverse impact, compliance, and lawsuit are also frequently associated with diversity programs. One of the most common misconceptions about diversity is that it is only Affirmative Action (AA) or Equal Employment Opportunity (EEO) although this is not true; EEO, AA and diversity efforts are not mutually exclusive and can ideally support one another. One thing is clear that both EEO and AA are primarily legally driven. EEO groups are people affected by past or continuing disadvantage or discrimination in employment. As a result they may be more likely to be unemployed or working in lower paying jobs. These groups are, women, aboriginal people, members of racial, ethnic, and ethno-religious minority groups and people with a disability. Furthermore, Equal Opportunity and Affirmative Action focus on disadvantaged groups, and the characteristics which these groups share, while the key assumption underlying Diversity Management is that all individuals are unique.[200] If a group of senior managers had been asked ten years ago to say how important equal opportunity issues were to business performance, some would not have seen the link. The intervening time has brought considerable change. EEO and AA are more of a business issue today and one key indicator in the number of chief executives who now understand and articulate a business case for diversity. However, those of us who have observed this new environment feel that the pace of change has been painfully slow. In case of EEO, the goal of equal opportunities is in terms of social justice and of redressing past wrongs, i.e. to correct an imbalance, an injustice and a mistake.[213] Quite apart from issues of equity, it means that service recipients should feel more comfortable and in some cases service is dealt with in their mother tongue. When we talk of organizations, the fundamental purpose of the equal opportunities framework and practices in organizations has been described in terms of the search for equality, i.e. the creation of conditions where women and men are treated the same and are not advantaged or disadvantaged because of their gender.[176]

Organizations operating with the Equal Opportunity paradigm translate it into organizational policies which are concerned often minimally with process, as to whether they have acted in the right way. Thus they may meet their formal legal obligations but only little more. Underlying the Equal Opportunity paradigm is the model of the organization as a rational, even-handed structure, operating fairly and dispensing justice and Equal Opportunity which neither changes nor seriously challenges this model. EEO is a basically a form a passive non-discrimination where all human resource management decision are made without regard to race, sex, religion, etc. —instead the decision is based on merit.

AFFIRMATIVE ACTION

Affirmative action in employment may be called as "hiring by the numbers" because of its focus on increasing the representation of the designated groups through targeted hiring, and to a lesser extent, training and promotion. It is a policy intended to deal directly and expeditiously with the *de facto* or systemic discrimination that remains embedded in policies and everyday practices in organizations and that reflects the historical legacy of *de jure* discrimination and exclusion. Affirmative action policy represents a commitment to end discrimination as a primary value which is not subordinated to other values.[82] Affirmative action originated in the USA in the mid-1960s to early 1970s as a response to deeply entrenched patterns of racial discrimination in institutions of employment and education, and the resulting exclusion, segregation and disadvantage of the black people. Under federal regulation, employers who received contracts, grants and other benefits from the US government were required to collect and report data on the composition of their workforce and to set goals and timetables for hiring in order to improve the representation of disadvantaged groups that were underrepresented relative to relevant labor markets. These groups included women, black people, Hispanics, Asians and American Indians. (Persons with disabilities are now covered under The Americans with Disabilities Act, 1991) Compliance with affirmative action hiring requirements was enforced in the 1970s, although not effectively or vigorously according to some critics. Civil rights complaints, litigation, and costly settlements of discrimination cases also impressed on employers the need to prevent discrimination and to implement affirmative action.

Affirmative Action and EEO were designed to eliminate barriers certain groups faced and combat racism and prejudice in hiring practices. In defending against prejudice, EEO denied difference among people. Being different was equated with being inferior. Therefore, equal rights came to mean that everyone is to be treated the same, with equal access and opportunity. Following paras throws light on the Affirmative Action Laws in USA:

- The Equal Pay Act of 1963 — requires every employer to pay employees equal salaries for equal work. It is currently administered by the Equal Employment Opportunity Commission (EEOC).

- Title VI of the Civil Rights Act of 1964 — prohibits discrimination based on race, color, or national origin in all programs or activities which receive federal financial aid. Employment discrimination is prohibited if a primary purpose of federal assistance is provision of employment (apprenticeship, training, work study or similar programs) or if program beneficiaries suffer unequal treatment because of hiring or assignment of counselors, trainers, faculty, or others in organizations receiving federal funds. Title VI is administered by the Office of Civil Rights, United States Department of Education.

- The Civil Rights Act of 1964 — Title VII prohibits employers, employment agencies and unions from discriminating on the basis of race, color, religion, sex or national origin. It is administered by the EEOC.

- The Rehabilitation Act of 1973 (Sections 503 and 504) — prohibits job discrimination on the basis of a physical or mental handicap, provided the applicant is otherwise qualified for the position. Also, employers are required to actively recruit qualified handicapped persons as part of an established affirmative action program. The Act is administered by the United States Department of Labor.

- Section 402 of the Vietnam Era Veterans Readjustment Assistance Act of 1974 — prohibits discrimination against any person because he or she is a disabled veteran of the Vietnam era. Employers are required to take affirmative action to enhance veteran's employment opportunities.

- Executive Order 11246 (Revised Order #4) — seeks

to promote and insure equal opportunity for all persons without regard to race, color, religion, sex or national origin of employees or persons seeking employment with government contractors. The Order is administered by the Office of Federal Contract Compliance Program (OFCCP), United States Department of Labor. It is this order that mandates that Affirmative Action Programs be described in written plans, with specific goals and timetables for recruiting, hiring, and upgrading blacks, other minorities and women.

- Title IX of the Education Amendments of 1972 — prohibits sex discrimination in any educational institution that receives federal assistance. Title IX is administered by the Office of Civil Rights, United States Department of Education.

- The Age Discrimination in Employment Act of 1967 — prohibits employers from discriminating against persons 40 years of age and over in any area of employment because of age.

- Immigration Reform and Control Act of 1986 — prohibits employers with more than three employees from discriminating based on citizenship or intending citizenship status and bars employers with more than three employees that aren't otherwise covered by Title VII from discriminating based on national origin. The Act is administered by the United States Department of Justice.

- State Law Against Discrimination, Ohio Revised

Code 4112.0 — prohibits discrimination in Ohio by reason of age, sex, handicap, color, religion, age, national origin, or ancestry in housing, public accommodation and employment. This law is administered by the Ohio Civil Rights Commission.

- The National Labor Relations Act and Related Laws — discrimination on the basis of race, religion or national origin may violate other rights under these laws. It may be unlawful for employers to participate with unions in a manner which gives rise to racial or other divisions among employees, to the detriment of organized union activity; or for unions to exclude individuals discriminatorily from union membership, thereby causing them to lose non-members in collective bargaining, processing of grievances, or to cause or attempt to cause employers to enter into discriminatory agreements.

When we talk of countries other than USA, unlawful discrimination occurs mostly at the time of hiring, during employment and at the point of termination. The legislation that complaints are based on operate though the creation of specialist tribunals. Affirmative action has been mandatory in Australia for almost a decade and now applies to about 3,000 of the country's largest employers. The rationale was that anti-discrimination laws must be complemented by positive steps both to counteract the continuing impact of past discrimination on women and migrants and to achieve change in social attitudes.

Australia's anti-discrimination and Affirmative Action laws are relatively recent compared to the USA. Beginning in the 1970s, federal and state governments, with the exception of Tasmania, enacted legislation prohibiting discrimination in employment based on sex, race and other grounds. As in many other countries, sex discrimination legislation followed a legislation against racial discrimination, a reflection of the later development of debate about the position of women in society. While the structure of Australian legislation differs among the jurisdictions the provisions have mainly three following common characteristics.

a)   Direct and indirect discrimination in employment is prohibited on specified grounds — Direct discrimination in the same position, for example by denying access to training opportunities. Indirect discrimination occurs as a result of imposing some conditions or requirement with which a person is not able to comply, whereas substantially greater number of persons of different sex or other specified characteristics would be able to comply. The breadth of this concept was demonstrated in Australian Iron and Steel v. Banovic (1989) 64 ALJ 51. In the case, the High Court found that a face value neutral retrenchment policy of last on, first off, was discriminatory as it perpetuated the effect of past discrimination. The Australian concept of direct discrimination corresponds to disparate treatment under Title VII of the United States Civil Rights Act, 1964, while indirect discrimination parallels the categories of adverse impact and perpetuating the effect of past discrimination.

b) The unlawfulness of indirect discrimination turns on its reasonableness — An authoritative statement of the meaning of this term has been provided in full by the Federal Court in Secretary, Department of Foreign Affairs v. Styles (1989) 88. ALJR 621. 635.

c) All jurisdictions prohibits discrimination on the grounds of sex, marital status, race, pregnancy and physical or mental impairment — Political opinion, family responsibilities or parental status, age, and sexual preference may also constitute grounds for unlawful discrimination in some of the jurisdictions. Significantly, in view of the overriding force of federal legislation, family responsibilities are included among the prohibited grounds of discrimination at the federal level.

In Canada there has been a significant backlash against federal and provincial policies on employment equity. This has been expressed in editorials and articles as well as in the repeal of Ontario's employment equity legislation, in political campaigns in other provinces, and in the politics of the Reform party at the federal level.

Some of the organizations use AA to monitor and control the changing demographics of their organization. Because, it affects hiring and promotion decisions, it is legally driven, benefits specific target groups, assumes that groups brought into the organization will adapt to prevailing norms and meets resistance due to fears of reverse discrimination and the limitations it imposes on autonomy in decision making. In Canada, the Employment Equity Act and the Federal Contractors Program, promulgated in 1986, were drawn in similar ways to the American affirmative action. These acts aimed at achieving a broad scope not only by improving the numerical representation, through recruiting, but also by promoting fairer employment systems, and trying to influence the discriminatory cultural patterns existent in organizations. Economic growth is a precondition to success of these programs and legislation is a necessary but not sufficient, condition for success.[70] While studying implementation of EEO in Australia, it came to the light that an unusual feature of the Australian situation was the role played by the system of compulsory conciliation and arbitration. Until recently, industrial relations and equal opportunity legislation operated in isolation from each other. Major amendments to legislation were designed to make the arbitral system a key instrument for advancing equity at work. While the conventional complaints based approach remained in place it was supplemented by a more interventionist approach. At the level of implementation, larger organizations responded to the legislative regime by developing equal opportunity and affirmative action policies. For smaller organizations, affirmative action and, to lesser extent, equal opportunity, remained problematic.[183] A number of studies on the effects of affirmative action and consent decree requirements have shown that organizations subject to them employed proportionally more blacks and white women than did comparable non-contractors in selected job categories (managerial, skilled trades, law enforcement, fire fighting, professions, the military), and that these groups' incomes increased. Affirmative action also contributed to growth in the number of small businesses owned by black entrepreneurs.[209] Affirmative Action is understood to imply quotas and a violation of principles of merit, it recommended the agency and its legislation be renamed as The Equal Opportunity for Women in the Workplace Agency. Structural changes have responded to another business criticism that "the current administration of the Act is too far removed from the realities of industry and that the agency operates in isolation from other stakeholders". Finally due to changes such as de-regulation, restructuring and globalization, "the goal posts have shifted since the Act was designed". Taken together, these changes "have all meant equity for women in the workplace is now a strategic human resource management issue". However, affirmative action was not designed to address the issue of integrating and retaining the racial minorities, women and other groups hired under its requirements. Focusing as it did on numerical representation, affirmative action compliance did not emphasize changing organizational policies, practices and climate in order to ensure that, once hired, members of the designated groups would be full and equal participants in the workplace, enjoying equitable career development opportunities and rewards for their contributions. In fact there is evidence that this has not happened, and that continuing discrimination and harassment — including white male backlash — have contributed to job dissatisfaction and turnover among affirmative action groups.[3] The evidence from US companies is that around 40 per cent have some sort of diversity management programme and that such programmes have had beneficial effects such as helping reduce stereotyping, fostering better relations and reducing workplace turnover. Some of these effects might be quite different from outcomes originally intended: as levers for improving workplace harmony and efficiency rather than improving work opportunities for the traditionally excluded.[3]

The contrast between equal opportunities and managing diversity is in perspective. On the one hand, equal opportunities can be largely perceived as an operational issue, which is likely to be the concern of personnel departments or human resource specialists. However, on the other hand, managing diversity as conceptualized can be regarded as a strategic issue in the widest sense, which is viewed as being crucial for economic and competitive success Furthermore; it is the concern of all employees[176], particularly managers, and not just those who are personnel or human resource managers. In addition, diversity management requires top leadership support, commitment and, above all, direction as it should theoretically extend beyond the more legal compliance-orientated equal opportunities.[76] In contrast to Affirmative Action and EEO, managing diversity sprang from a business-defined imperative and a management framework. "Valuing diversity" programmes were soon superseded by the more active "managing diversity", the two approaches differentiated, according to proponents, by the extent to which differences are seen as a source of competitive advantage.[213]

Global Air has a long history of EEO and diversity management going back to the later 1980s, which contrast quite strongly with other manufacturing companies. Senior managers demonstrated a strong commitment to EEO and diversity management, and awareness training was "mainstreamed" through many areas of HR policy such as recruitment and selection, and performance review. The long-standing involvement in EEO and diversity management meant that there was considerable effort devoted to systematic auditing of staff, producing a breakdown by grade, job, and site the basis of gender, ethnicity, disability, and type of employment contact (but not age and sexual orientation), and to ensure that the organization complied with the law. However, there was not evidence that these data were integrated with that held in relation to other aspects of HR policy such as access to training and development, appraisal outcomes, labor turnover and sickness absence. There were however EEO and diversity "champions" and consultative forums located in different departments, and for different categories of staff.

In India the Constitution of India provides for affirmative action through job reservations and these are based on caste plus socio-economic backwardness. Governments — both central and state — also have fixed quotas for women, schedule caste, schedule tribes and other backward castes, disabled, ex-army personnel, etc.

in education and employment in the government sector. So far, such reservations are restricted to government run or government-aided institutions and not the private sector as such. On several occasions, to woo concerned interest groups, both the central and several state governments showed a tendency to increase the reservations for one or more sections of society to influence their voting patterns.[225] The Indian constitution seeks to establish an enlightened and egalitarian society. It gave its women adult franchise and property rights, equal access to education, and equal right to run for public office. The laws do not discriminate against women. Management processes and diversity form top management perspective.

7

Diversity Management and HR Interventions

Workforce diversity is a present day necessity for future clarity and efficiency of all organizations. In order to make this work we need strategies and multiple ways to make each organization become a multicultural workplace. This process begins with the top leaders of the organization, as well as an effort put forth from all employees. "Diversity is a commitment from senior managers; the budget and staff downsizing; the difficulty of attracting minorities; the scarcity of minorities with the skills required; and finally, resistance of some groups to working with staff from diverse backgrounds". All of these constraints are real problems that we have in our society. Therefore, we need to find ways around this negative attitude. Some strategies involve equal employment opportunity and affirmative action.[44]

TRAINING PROGRAMMES ON DIVERSITY

The effective integration of diverse group members also require high quality "diversity training". Diversity training is, unfortunately, not always underpinned by frameworks and guidelines from valid social research.[181] Unless training programmes facilitate a real understanding and appreciation of most diversity management issues, they are unlikely to have a positive impact in the workplace. Organizational training interventions do successfully tackle negative attitudes towards diversity. Such intervention may develop unrealistic views about the role that diversity plays within any workplace and leave more problematic diversity issues unmentioned and unmanaged.[183] All employees should be provided an opportunity to become actively involved in a continuous learning process for their professional and personal enhancement. The more each employee knows, the greater the development of skill level, the more significant and effective can be their contribution toward the attainment of corporate goals. Often, companies are tempted to provide training opportunities to the upper and mid-level, while overlooking first line personnel. Such a practice discourages rather than aids the grooming process of "hands-on" employees for promotional opportunities.[180]

Most of the time diversity training programmes are usually voluntary initiatives for employers who have total discretion as to how they will be implemented. Although the decision to implement the training is often made or approved at the top of the organization, the participation of top management appears to be rare. Diversity training is usually targeted to middle managers, first line supervisors, and specialized functions such as customer service, in which improved communication and "human relations" skills are expected to result in bottom line benefits. Blue collar, clerical and technical workers are much less likely to be involved in the training.[29] The major drawbacks to most existing diversity training programs are (a) they do not build skills to facilitate individuals' ability to actually manage their interactions with individuals different from themselves (b) they are not rigorous nor time-intensive enough to create a paradigm shift in individuals' treatment toward individuals different from themselves and (c) there are no enduring reinforcement mechanisms embedded in the organization's culture to ensure all individuals' inputs are successfully managed to meet the organization's strategic goals. As a result, most (if not all) existing diversity programs have not been successful in creating enduring changes in the way individuals interact with individuals different from themselves, nor have they been successful in changing their organization's culture to one that systemically manages diversity. In order to creates enduring change in individuals and the organization's culture, members of the organization at all levels need to participate in diversity training that encapsulates the comprehensive managing diversity process. The outcomes that should be expected from participation include, but are not limited to, skill building in the following areas: the ability to clearly articulate their ideas and feelings; conflict management skills; effective giving and receiving of feedback; effective listening; group observation skills; and group decision-making skills, all of which will facilitate modified attitudes and behaviors, and healthy interaction with diverse individuals. Individuals have to come to grips with their feelings, thoughts, attitudes, and behaviors toward diversity and others with whom they are different. In the first step of Exposure, individuals provide public notice of where they are at that point. They do this by: laying open who they are; divulging where they are from; unmasking themselves; and receiving others' culture.[118]

Much of the current literature shows that there are challenges to the development of awareness-based training initiatives. Current literature is also littered with examples of awareness-based training interventions that not only failed to achieve their goals, but further polarized diverse groups at work, making their future integration even more difficult than before. It is also important to recognize that organizationally driven diversity training is inherently constrained by being only one of a range of sources of influence on the individuals who participate in them.[152]

If we take the example of an Australian workforce, an important barrier that affects full integration of ethnic employees is the issue of communication, mainly English literacy.[132] A number of steps must be taken by the management to ensure effectiveness in communication. For example, translating summaries of the documents into the main workplace languages, providing English language and literacy training for migrants, training migrant staff on workplace cultural issues and training all staff in cross-cultural communication are examples of such activities.[150]

HR trainers should introduce in design, diversity training programmes. Blakar's theory states that a broad competence for effective integration is achieved though the development of important communication skills. These skills are in turn based on the existence of some key preconditions: a shared social reality between group members; ability to "decentre" or to consider viewpoints that may differ from one's own; motivation to communicate, ability to negotiate and endorse contracts of behaviour and ability to attribute difficulties appropriately.

The content of diversity training usually includes information on changing demographics, and often about bias, prejudice and stereotypes, but not discrimination. Typically, training sessions should provide experiential and self assessment exercises and role playing, and some sessions on diverse cultures.[33] Central to an organization's repertoire of diversity management skills should be a competence for managing and analyzing organizational networks. They argue that a failure to understand the power of informal networks may lead to misguided attempts at diversity training and development. Unless participants in diversity training programmes can develop a robust understanding of how informal networks operate within their work contexts, they will be less able to influence and enhance such important processes as communication, information exchange and decision making processes.

INTERVENTION AT RECRUITMENT LEVEL

Since organizations often resort to internal promotions to fill vacancies, recruiting a diverse workforce at critical entry points to the organizations also ensure that a diverse pool of talent is available for promotion. To achieve these objectives, recruitments and selection processes must be based on organizational and job-relevant criteria and managers who run these processes should be skilled in assessing the criteria.[113] Managing growth in workforce diversity and increasing the representation of women and minorities throughout the organization is a critical strategic human resource (HR) management issue for most organizations.[212] Job qualification demands are discriminatory if they are not relevant to the position for which the candidate has applied. Interviewers are cautioned against any tendency to disqualify women and other minorities by relying on sexual or racial stereotypes. The stereotypes may include false assumptions about the sort of occupations deemed traditional and acceptable for women, the sort of work and time burdens that may be erroneously imposed on women, the ability of women or other minorities to maintain commitment to a job, the propriety of putting women in male dominated environments, and the assumed effects women or minorities may have on employee morale or on customers.[26] HR diversity change strategies that bring in many new hires of different backgrounds may have negative ramifications for social functioning in groups, particularly if new members are not supported by additional HR strategies that allow them to enter work groups on an equal footing or if their work groups do not have leadership that mirror their demographic identities. As it found, identity groups must be equal in their access to power resources if contact is to produce improvement in attitudes. There must also be time for the new members to be socialized and integrated into the culture.[115]

INTEGRATED CHANGE PRACTICES

Effective management of workforce diversity involves not just recruiting diverse employees but also retaining them. One way of increasing retention rates is by providing adequate training and development opportunities to employees. In the case of multicultural employees training may also assist in understanding special rules and regulations. Diverse employees often feel neglected and do not perceive any career paths. Employee development programs can address this problem, by preparing employees for future promotions.[45] It is increasingly being recognized that specific competencies and skills are necessary in order to work successfully as members of a diverse group. People who are not equipped with these will be less able to develop the integrating group processes that are characteristic of highly effective diverse groups. Developing integrating competencies and skills in a diverse group should not be an attempt to make it more homogeneous (although many training interventions have been criticized for being precisely that); rather these capacities should create a mechanism where individuals can retain their dimensions of diversity (which are inherently valuable for a variety of group tasks) while at the same time avoiding such damaging processes as dysfunctional interpersonal conflict, miscommunication, higher levels of stress, slower decision making and problems with group cohesiveness.[181]

Managing diversity also involves leveraging and using the cultural differences in people's skills, ideas and creativity to contribute to a common goal, and doing it in a way that gives the organization a competitive edge. Recent studies have shown a strong correlation between good diversity creativity, a wider range or perspectives, better problem definition, more alternatives and better solutions.[1] To reap these benefits, diversity must be managed effectively.[45] HR strategies to manage organizational demographic change which are socially constructed and enacted at the work group level. It is especially important to identify what constitutes a group level tipping point or critical mass across hierarchical levels and different demographic groups to enable positive consensus supporting change. HR strategies must increase diversity through hiring to alter tipping points within targeted work groups. This will dramatically alter the saliency of strategic organizational demographic change and intervene to shape the climate of specific units.[115]

According to cognitive theory, individuals construct meaning and make sense by building metal representations that guide their thinking and the direction of their decisions.[177]

It is found that if women are under-represented at higher organizational levels, relations between women at lower levels might be of lower quality due to increased competition and negative gender dynamics in the larger social system. If HR change strategies that alter the distribution of existing resources across organizational and demographic groups are to be successful, they must take into account how, not only tipping points in terms of overall departmental representation, but, more importantly, how tipping points are distributed in demographies across the hierarchies of work groups or departments.[63] In order to manage demographic change in economic and labor markets, a common HR change strategy is to increase the diversity of the work force through hiring over time. Though most HR strategies to manage diversity are conceived at the firm level, they are often socially and practically enacted at the work group level of analysis.[122]

Successful movement through the managing diversity process requires individuals to change. Resistance to change is inherent in any change process, and it will be no different in this process. Therefore, the managing diversity process is a fluid, continuous process that needs to be systematically reinforced and embedded in the organization's culture and individuals' interactions, such that the organization's culture and its members do not revert back to just acknowledging or valuing diversity. Hence, refreezing the desired state of managing diversity requires reinforcing the new perceptions, attitudes, and behaviors with emphasis on the modified behaviors and healthy interactions individuals have adopted as a result of going through the managing diversity process. In order for individuals and organizations not to revert back to their previous states, the new desired state must go through the refreezing stage to be institutionalized. This should be accomplished through systemic, on-going training and daily interactions at the individual level, and through revised policies, procedures, and systems at the organizational level.[183]

8

Best Practices in Managing Cultural Diversity

Successful management of today's increasingly diverse workforce is among the most important global challenges faced by corporate leaders, human resource managers, and management consultants. Workforce diversity is not a transient phenomenon; it is today's reality; and it is here to stay. Homogenous societies have become heterogeneous, and this trend is irreversible. The problem of managing today's diverse workforce, however, do not stem from the heterogeneity of the workforce itself but from the inability of corporate managers to fully comprehended its dynamics, diverse themselves of their personal prejudicial attitude and creative potential embedded in a multicultural workforce. Top Management of the corporate faces a number of challenges in attempting to maintain this balance, such as leadership, single work ethic, workplace authority, mentoring, new work configurations and work-life balance. Leaders need to achieve a balance between the human needs of diverse groups and the business objectives. Corporate leaders must focus on the implications of business decisions, policies, and practices on the diverse human component, the law, and the bottom line.[224]

Another challenge for the management of today is to have people from different cultures and ethnic backgrounds agree on a single work ethic. In addition to the impact of culture and ethnicity on achieving a single work ethic, leadership teams need to address differences such as age, business and personal experiences, education, family circumstances, gender, language, physical or mental ability or disability, organizational level, race, religion, and sexual orientation.[224] Even more challenging is creating professional agreement and understanding among people of different countries and religious traditions who have differing views about cultural diversity.

The literature on diversity highlights a range of responses to the challenges of diversity management[46] identified no fewer than twelve strategic responses to the challenge of managing diversity. Moore reduced the number of behavioural stereotypes to four — the diversity hostels, the diversity blind, the diversity naïve and the diversity integrationist. Whilst the first three behavior stereotypes fail to recognize that different management skills sets are required to respond effectively to different diversity challenges, the fourth stereotype is proactive in its approach. Moore's stereotypes recognize that neither functional nor cultural diversity automatically leads to positive or negative outcomes. However, different patterns of diversity present different managerial challenges, to which some organizations respond, whilst others do not.[149]

Studies on racio-ethnic diversity have also been mixed, although it reported more studies that found a negative effect of racio-ethnic diversity on performance as compared to a positive effect. Research studies offers a great deal of promise, showing that cultural diversity does add value, and that for companies using a growth strategy, diversity can lead to a competitive advantage. Others have argued for the positive impact that cultural diversity has for an organization in terms of advantages in resource allocation, marketing enhanced creativity, problem solving, and flexibility. [43]

While there may not be much empirical evidence to substantiate claims that effectively managed diversity directly leads to bottom-line increases, there is real-world evidence (e.g. Coca-Cola, Denny's, Publix, and Texaco settlements) to suggest that not effectively managing gender and racio-ethnic diversity has been, and can be, detrimental to organizations and their bottom lines. Thus, it is a logical extrapolation that an organization's ability or inability to create a culture in which diversity is systemically acknowledged, valued, and effectively managed is more likely to determine the affects diversity will have on its bottom line. The frameworks are presented for using a planned change-corporate diversity strategy to: advance from the initial passive states of acknowledging and valuing diversity to the final active state of managing diversity on the "diversity continuum"; and systemically manage diversity using the specific eight-step "managing diversity process".[59]

INCLUSION-EXCLUSION CONSTRUCT

Practitioners argue a culturally diverse workforce can bring broad perspectives to organizational issues, allowing problems to be approached from a wider variety of angels than might otherwise occur within a more homogenous workforce. Along similar lines, researchers have reported diverse work groups generate more creative ideas and are more productive, in the long run. Within the organizational context, the inclusion-exclusion construct is conceptualized as a continuum of the degree to which an individual feels as a part of critical organizational processes, such as access to information, connectedness to coworkers, and ability to participate in and influence the decision-making process. The importance of the inclusion-exclusion experience is the measure of a work organization's success at becoming a truly global company. Because people have always depended on one another for their livelihood and needed to work together in order to acquire food, shelter, and clothing, social inclusion had had an improvement survival functions through the ages and across cultures. Dynamic companies look for people who are different from us because the diverse workforce may bring different talents, interests, and viewpoints. The organizations which fail to embrace cultural diversity effectively and do not adopt a holistic approach to eliminate discrimination and injustice will adversely affect both employees and customers.[190]

UNLEARNING OF THE PRACTICES

To be successful, managers need to "unlearn" practices rooted in an old mind set, change the ways organizations operate, shift company culture, revise policies, create new structures, and redesign human resource systems. Diversity initiatives can improve the quality if an organization's workforce. Organizations spend a large sum of their budgets on human resources in the form of salaries, benefits, training development, and recruitment. In order to get a good return on their investment in human capital and maximize their competitive advantage, it is important to recognize that the workforce will grow in the number of women.[185] General Motors is a strong supporter of the Global Sullivan Principles. These principles have their roots in the 1977 Sullivan principles developed for South Africa by the late Reverend Leon H. Sullivan. These principles provide guidance to companies worldwide "regarding core issue such as human rights, worker rights, the environment, community relations, supplier relations, fair competitions". Reverend Sullivan was the first African American to be appointed to the Board of Directors of a major U.S. company when he accepted General Motors Invitation in 1971. The multicultural perspective seeks to provide a conceptual framework that recognizes the complex diversity of plural society while, at the same time, suggesting bridges of shared concern that bind culturally different persons to one another. From the last two decades, multiculturalism has become recognized as a powerful force, not just for understanding exotic groups but also for understanding ourselves and those with whom we work.

The approach traditionally taken to workforce diversity in organizations is a melting-pot approach — that is, it has been assumed that diverse individuals would want to and should assimilate. It has been observed, however, that people in fact do not set aside their cultural values, lifestyle preferences, and especially not their identities in working life. Organizations thus face the challenge of making themselves more sensitive to the diverse perspectives of different groups of people.

WORKFORCE DIVERSITY PRACTICES

Human resource managers are faced with the challenge of convincing their senior management that diversity programs are beneficial to the organization. Some organizational leaders are concerned that implementing diversity initiatives is too expensive, upsets productivity and causes disruption in the workforce. Prejudice and hostile work environments also pose internal stumbling blocks to managing workforce diversity effectively.

Diversity combined with an understanding of individual strength and weaknesses, and working relationships that are founded upon sensitivity and trust, have been shown to enhance creativity and problem-solving capability. The key factors that contribute to creativity and provide a collaborative climate include trust, team spirit, unified commitment, principled leadership, an elevating goal, a results-driven structure, standards of excellence, participation in decision-making, external support and recognition, and an aptitude to adjust roles and behaviours to accommodate new emergent values. Again, good workforce diversity practices in the area of human resources, are believed to enhance employee and organizational performance. Diversity practices involves leveraging and using the cultural differences in people's skills, ideas and creativity to contribute to a common goal, and doing it in a way that gives the organization a competitive edge. Recent studies have shown a strong correlation between good diversity creativity, a wider range or perspectives, better problem definition, more alternatives and better solutions. To reap these benefits, diversity must be managed effectively. One study reports that the single most important factor in taking corrective action is to get the attention of the CEO. Other steps may hold top management accountable for maintaining a diverse organization, create internal advocacy groups, identify women in the leadership succession process and provide workers of "protected groups" with opportunities for start-up and trouble-shooting assignments. Senior management attempts to embrace women and other minorities into the ranks of upper management must be deliberate rather than accidental.[150] It has also been purported that if diversity can be effectively managed in an organization, some potential benefits to the organization include greater creativity and innovation, and improved decision-making. Conversely, if diversity is not managed effectively, some potential major costs to the organization include, at a minimum, breakdowns in communication, interpersonal conflict, and higher turnover.[43]

It is argued that diversity in terms of ethnicity, age, gender, personality and educational background promotes creativity and problem-solving capability. However, that groups have been found to be less risk averse than an individual's "risky shift". Increased diversity leads to lower levels of risk aversion and better decision-making and problem-solving capability. This arises because diversity promotes a more robust critical evaluation of the fist solution to receive substantial support. Many organizations in Australia conduct blanket literacy and language testing in recruitment. These tests bear no relationship to the specific job requirements. In addition, interviewers have little or no understanding of techniques suitable for interviewing applicants from different ethnic backgrounds. Effective management of diversity recognizes that people from different backgrounds, culture and experiences can bring new ideas to the workforce. Several "best practices" have been recommended to improve management of workforce diversity in the area of recruitment and selection. These include the development of a job description and selection process that cover job relevant duties, qualifications, and experience and complies with anti-discrimination legislation. Other practices include attracting applications to daily newspapers, presence of diverse managers on selection committees and implementing techniques that allow diverse people to answer questions to the best of their ability and potential. Interviews constitute an important part of the selection process.

Procter & Gamble in 1988 formed a Corporate Diversity Strategy Task Force to clarify the concept of diversity, define its importance for the company and identify strategies for making progress toward successfully managing a diverse work force. The basic idea behind this is to practice the gender diversity including the cultural diversity and that to expand its view of the value of differences. P&G is now conducting a thorough, continuing evaluation of all management programs to be sure that systems are working well for everyone. It has also carried out a corporate survey to get a better picture of the problems facing P&G employees who are balancing work and family responsibilities and to improve company programs in such areas as dependent care. Xerox is another organization which believes that a firm and resolute commitment to affirmative action is the first and most important step to work force diversity. In mid-1960s Xerox began recruiting minorities and women systematically. The company's approach emphasizes behavior expectations. Xerox managed in three different ways. Firstly, give emphasis on workforce demography by recruitment and representation in upper level jobs according to federal laws. Secondly, provide scope to women and minorities for upward mobility and thirdly, enhancing of personal relationship by knowing each other well. The role of line managers is pivotal in implementing a managing diversity approach; however, this category of staff is apparently under particular pressure in the organizational interpretation and application of managing diversity. Unless and until organizations formally offers direction in its managing diversity approach, it seems likely that their line managers will be less than proactive in this area.[76] Human resource practices from top to bottom need to be re-examine to cope with the new strengths and challenges of diversity, so better approaches can be created by management to recruit new talent, retain them, and manage them more effectively.

DIVERSITY STRATEGY AND GOAL OF ORGANIZATION

Diversity must be part of an organization's strategic business objective. Diversity goals must be linked to business goals, not just meeting affirmative action of legal requirements. Diversity must be stressed internally as well as externally through outreach programs within the community.[185] Companies should rethink and redefine missions, strategies, management practices, cultures, markets, and products to meet the needs of an increasingly diverse body of employees, customers and stakeholders.[6] Ultimately, the key to create, develop, and retain a diverse workforce is to find a way to make the workforce feel connected to their company.[65] The first type of strategy integration that must occur is that of diversity strategy with the overall mission of the organization. For profit-making companies, the task also involves clarifying the impact of managing diversity on profitability. The challenge for leaders is to clearly communicate the details of how the potential performance benefit of diversity specifically applies to an organization.

When we talk of strategy, the first type of strategy integration that must occur is that of diversity strategy with the overall mission of the organization. For profit-making companies, the task also involves clarifying the impact of managing diversity on profitability. The challenge for leaders is to clearly communicate the details of how the potential performance benefit of diversity specifically applies to an organization. David Karpin who led the Industry Taskforce on Leadership and Management Skills focused on the need to create and develop internationally competitive organization in Australia. He analyzed Australia's attempts to manage diversity as a lost wealth creating opportunity by Australian managers due to their lack of vision or ability to harness the talent of women and ethnic people in the workplace. A number of studies have identified the critical areas of successful strategies to lead today's diverse workforce. The identified areas for strategy formulation and implementation are recruitment, selection, and retention; supplier diversity; communications including mission, advertising, public relations, and websites; compliance; assessment, training, and career development, including mentoring; and compensation and benefits including rewards and recognition.[224]

HR managers must solicit a trainable population, check required skills and competencies against the job, market jobs sufficiently ahead of need, and extend the workforce boundaries to include the nationals of other countries. Organizations which plan for the anticipated workforce and accept cultural diversity management as a progressive technique will benefit from better employee retention, increased productivity, less absenteeism, better morale, an expanded marketplace and improved customer service. Since employees are typically hired and are expected to assimilate into departments, it is important to understand how demographic changes are experienced in this context. Departmental groups are the receptacles of organizational dispersion of HR strategies to manage diversity. Individuals are embedded in departmental work groups, which provide a context shaping the social meaning of HR strategies to shift organizational demography. Research is mixed on whether HR strategies to increase minority representation results in positive or negative group processes, depending on whether one takes a social contact.[2] A strategic human resource plan that includes a number of different strategies to enhance diversity and promote the productivity and effectiveness of the workforce. Human resource managers must solicit a trainable population, check required skills and competencies against the job, market jobs sufficiently ahead of need, and extend the workforce boundaries to include the nationals of other countries. Organizations which plan for the anticipated workforce and accept cultural diversity management as a progressive technique will benefit from better employee retention, increased productivity, less absenteeism, better morale, an expanded marketplace and improved customer service.

GENDER SENSITIVITY

While networks can provide sources of support for the individuals in them, they also allow women to act in concert, lessening the risk to any one individual of pointing out systemic issues, requesting resources to address equity issues or taking other proactive steps to change organizational culture.[224] The identification and development of high-potential employees is a crucial element of organizational development at any company intent on maximizing performance. In order to leverage the intellectual capital of the entire workforce, it is essential that these processes are inclusive of female talent. This is not to suggest that women are excluded explicitly, but it is essential that talent identification processes do not discriminate against differing work styles and work experiences, and instead concentrate on identifying talent in all its forms. No one can be defined as different in isolation. It is only against the background of a variety of contextual factors that it is possible to evaluate the extent to which they appear similar to or different from the people in their environment. A lone female among a group of males, for example, is more likely to be defined according to her gender than would otherwise be the case. Research has shown that individuals choosing non traditional roles at work e.g. female construction workers generally require additional "bolstering" in the form of particular personality traits (e.g. higher levels of self esteem) or through supplemental support from their organization.[87]

Gender, as a dimension of diversity, is strongly

associated with job segregation with women's work and men's work being highly segregated according to both job types and organizational level. Occupational statistics demonstrate that there is a persistently unequal distribution of males and females throughout all ranges of occupations, and that this is an almost world-wide phenomenon. Males and females are both segregated into (and over-represented in) particular organizational roles and levels of authority. Management can take a variety of steps to display their commitment to welcoming the culturally diverse workforce. Options may include increasing the presence of women and other minorities on corporate boards and executive positions.

CROSS-CULTURAL AND GENDER SPECIFIC TRAINING

The basic problem facing leaders is how to describe behavior in terms that true to particular culture while at the same time comparing those behaviors with a similar pattern in one or more other cultures. Combining the specific and general viewpoints provides a multicultural perspective. This larger perspective is an essential starting point for leaders seeking to avoid cultural encapsulation by their own culture-specific assumption. Developing multicultural awareness, knowledge, and skills is not an end in itself, but rather a means toward increasing a person's power, energy, and freedom of intentional choices in a multicultural and diverse world. Multicultural awareness, knowledge and skills increase a person's intentional and purposive decision-making ability by accounting for the many ways that culture influences different perceptions of the same solution. Increasing multicultural awareness has real, tangible outcomes. Research has found that resumes randomly assigned White sounding names such as Emily Walsh and Brendan Baker resulted in 50% more interview than resumes assigned African American-sounding names such as Lakisha Washington and Jamal Jones. Apart from their names, the resumes, which depicted phantom job seekers, showed the same experience, education, and skills. Another finding was that the likelihood of being called back for an interview rose significantly with credentials like experience and honors for White-sounding names much more than for Black-sounding names. Having an awareness of unconscious biases that may be affecting the status of a job applicant is the first step to a fair equitable selection process that hires applicants based on true ability and not perceived ability.

To be effective, senior management needs to agree on and hold people accountable for the measures of success. A study done by the Corporate Leadership Council CLC found that candidate and top talent tracking and employee surveys are the most commonly used measures, and companies are starting to look at tracking hiring, retention and promotion statistics over time (diversity scorecards) as a measure of success, looking either for continuous improvement or progress toward articulated goals. Managers should also be held accountable for making sure that women and people of color are compensated at the same level as their white male peers. Embracing diversity should be made everyone's challenge, and in everyone's best interest. It is a senior management who can make this state a reality.

DEVELOPING DIVERSITY SPECIFIC ORGANIZATIONAL CULTURE

There are eight preconditions that help to position organizations to use identity-group difference in the service of organizational learning, growth, and renewal. The leadership must understand that a diverse workforce will embody different perspective and approaches to work, and must truly value variety of opinion and insight. The leadership must recognize both the learning opportunities and the challenges that the expression of different perspectives presents for an organization.

The organizational culture must create an expectation of high standards of performance from everyone. The organizational culture must stimulate personal development. The organizational culture must encourage openness. The culture must make workers feel valued. The organization must have a well-articulated and widely understood mission. The organization must have a relatively egalitarian, non-bureaucratic structure.

On the other hand some organizational cultures are more positive and supportive of diversity than others. The broad approaches to diversity within organizations identifies accompanying attitudes, and their implications for organizational development and training and accordingly organizations can be parochial (diversity blind), ethnocentric (diversity hostile) or synergistic (diversity integrating).[89]

Organizations are increasing surface (demographic) and deep level (attitudinal) diversity simultaneously, which is likely to have negative short-term ramifications for the consensus and direction of climate. HR strategies must not only focus on the surface level — reflecting structural and demographic attributes — but also simultaneously to deep level characteristics reflecting values within the context of specific groups at all organizational levels. HR strategists and change agents must focus on how HR change strategies relate to the joint alignment of group member's multiple characteristics (e.g. demographic, hierarchical status, task) in work groups — that is, to examine group contextual influences.[232] Recent research has also revealed that diversity itself does not drive productivity. Rather, network density (the frequency of team member communication) and network heterogeneity (the proportion of that communication that occurs among diverse members of the team) are associated with productivity.[168]

Management practices are needed that encourage a learning culture that embraces all employees regardless of the cultural similarity with their leaders. It is assumed, often incorrectly, that leaders with global skills will likely have multicultural awareness, knowledge, and skills. Unfortunately, 85% of Fortune 500 firms believe there are insufficient numbers of employees with global leadership skills. According to the Center for Global Assignments survey, even when employees do posses global leadership skills, 60% said they are inadequate for their organizations' needs. Interestingly, although leadership is seen as an important fact for global growth, only 8% of executives and managers rated their organizatiqn's overall leadership capacity as excellent, while nearly one half (47%) rated this capacity to be only fair or poor. Thus, there seems to be a disconnect between the incorporate of leadership and culturally related issues and the current leadership capacity available.

Managing diversity involves leveraging and using the cultural differences in people's skills, ideas and creativity to contribute to a common goal, and doing it in a way that gives the organization a competitive edge. Recent studies have shown a strong correlation between good diversity creativity, a wider range or perspectives, better problem definition, more alternatives and better solutions.

MENTORING AND NURTURING LEADERSHIP

The development of networks, mentors and role models for diverse group members is an important dimension of organizational development initiatives designed to support and manage diversity. The majority groups may display a range of defensive behaviours which can obstruct the participation or performance of those in the minority. This also suggests that minority/ diverse groups will be less likely themselves to engage in concerted efforts to challenge existing stereotypes at work. If those to whom definitions of diversity apply most strongly are not inspired by people they perceive to be similar to themselves, it appears that it will be less likely that they will feel psychologically or practically equipped to achieve certain goals, to occupy certain positions, or to play certain roles at work.[140] In many of these of companies with successful tack records in developing diverse talent, the CEO is directly involved, in developing diverse talent.

The fundamental components of effective leadership in a culturally diverse society are a knowledge base which increases sensitivity to and awareness of the diversities in the workforce, identification of resources which can strengthen and improve the quality of life for diverse individuals, open communication with others about cultural differences, and strategies which will enable leaders to serve as change agents to maximize the benefits of a culturally diverse workforce.[224] Leaders need to develop multicultural awareness, knowledge, and skills to respond appropriately to the problems and opportunities of both domestic demographic changes in globalization. The leader who is an effective, committed champion of diversity may need the skills of great leadership, defined as (a) the ability to engage others in shared meaning (b) a distinctive and compelling voice (c) a sense of integrity (d) adaptive capacity and (e) an ability to conquer a negative situation and emerge stronger.

An effective leader in a culturally embedded organization can evoke cultural symbols, myths, mythological themes, rituals and religious ideas to create vision and mission for the organization which can then motivate and inspire the subordinates to rise above their narrow selfishness and to give their best to the organization. The reports of Fiji, India, and Iran contain a number of examples where cultural ethos were utilized to maintain a high level of productivity.

THE LEAST FUNCTIONAL STRATEGY

Many organizations have implemented various diversity initiatives as a part of their corporate diversity strategy, but most have not used a planned change approach to strategically align their initiatives with their long-term objectives and strategic positioning.[121] It is highly probable that this lack of planned strategic alignment contributes immensely to the purported ineffectiveness of many diversity initiatives. The least functional strategy or adjustment for dealing with diversity issues in companies is called separation. Separation involves rejecting all cultural values except your own. This can be thought of as a form of alienation. This of course causes a great deal of conflict between coworkers from different cultural backgrounds. Assimilation and deculturation fall between multiculturalism and separation. Assimilation is the adoption of the organization's culture. This is usually seen by subordinate groups as conforming to the values of the dominant group. This strategy often produces mistrust in the long run if the dominant group does not attempt to understand the values of the subordinate groups. Finally, deculturation is viewed as a weak or benign from of separation that occurs when all groups maintain their own value without trying to influence anyone else. One example would be an expatriate who does not understand an employee's culture and has no desire to change that situation.

REPORTING OF DIVERSITY PRACTICES

The content and frameworks for reporting diversity vary greatly, and this makes it hard to compare different companies. Some provide data such as the number of women employed in the company; others do not. Some describe which groups are encompassed by the term "diversity"; other do not. A few report on different diversity initiatives in detail; most do not do this. Another issue is about the scope of diversity. Where diversity is mentioned it is most likely to be about staff. It is therefore hard to know whether companies are unaware of diversity in its broader sense, such as with regard to suppliers and customers, or whther they are simply not reporting on this. Similarly, initiatives to create a culture which celebrates diversity (e.g. such as a global diversity task force) are by no means universal. Again, the question is whether they are simply not reported upon or not happening at all? Certainly some companies might be termed "minimalists" in terms of diversity reporting. They may briefly mention the term diversity in a section on HR or employees section, but provide little more. Others provide short description of individual projects or three or four internet pages and references to partner organizations, but do not provide any information about a "vision" or strategic plan. One company publishes a CSR report which focuses only on community and environmental issues, thereby excluding HR and diversity issues. These may be mentioned elsewhere, such as a part of graduate web site data, but there is no signposting and few signs of any standard approach.

9

Diversity Management – The Indian Perspective

The manifestation of "care" vary in culturally embedded and multinational organizations. In the former, the nature of caring behavior and the feeling of being cared are determined by cultural imperatives. Because employees value familial and personalized relationships, like to obey and respect paternalistic superiors, prefer to depend on them for guidance, directions, affection, nurturance, patronage, and so on, the superior should meet these expectations in order to let the subordinates feel that the superior cares. "One important Indian ethos, that is the norm in the organization, is respect for elders and seniors. Commitment with elders and seniors is expected to nurture, guide and develop their juniors and subordinates down the line." A leader in Indian organization quite often uses affection, guidance, and direction for those subordinates who prefers dependency, personalized, and status-oriented relationships in order to make them work hard. The leader also spends a good deal of his time on the shop floor to maintain his or her visibility. The essential components of such leadership are explicit role expectations, paternalistic care, and patronage to the subordinates, which then are instrumental for their productive behavior.

According to Indian researchers, there are a number of traditional and relatively contemporary sources of the dominant Indian values. The main traditional sources are the Hindu religion, the caste system of social stratification, and the agricultural mode of production which have jointly given rise to an asset of highly idealized moral values of religio-philosphical nature. They were tempted by centuries of event and experiences to appear as social values, the dominant among them being a preferences for (a) arranging ideas, persons, relationships, and all other conceivable tangible and intangible things hierarchically, (b) maintaining personalized relationships, (c) adopting a moralistic orientation to discharge duties and meet obligations to the family, friends and relatives, and d) maintaining harmony and tolerance among in-group members. These value are attributed to the colonial rule in India. The colonial model of bureaucracy, for example, brought on an ethos of mistrust of the natives, and thereby strengthened the value of hierarchy by emphasizing highly centralized modes of decision making, maintaining a large power distance, and refusing to delegate authority to subordinates. The British rule also degraded the economy and limited the access to education to a few. This resulted in pervasive poverty, mass illiteracy, over-population, and badly deficient infrastructure. Frequent epidemics, flood, famines, and other natural calamities injected a high degree of uncertainly, insecurity and a sense of acute scarcity of resources, which in turn induced a short-time perspective. It is observed that most Indians live physically in the present, but psychologically in the past, and are unconcerned about the future. Against this background, the country imported Western capital and technology to industrialize fast and catch up with the West. As a part of this package, organizations adopted Western systems of management. Institutions arranged management education accordingly. It was also seen that the Western style of management education, industrial experience, and modernization in Indian promoted individualistic and egalitarian values.

In case of Indian managers, it was found out like their Western counterparts, they underplayed the importance of Indian social values (such as social relationships and interactions) and professed to value achievement, advancement, ability utilization, perusal development, and so on. It seems that Indians have acquired both indigenous and Western values. While the indigenous values are transmitted through primary socialization and sustained by social institution, the Western values are cultivated through management education and maintained by job demands in work organizations.

The common refrain about India is that "it is such a diverse country whatever you say of it, the opposite is equally true". In India you will find "a society that has, like Europe's, the diversities of a continent and the unities of a civilization". Such is the measure of the magnitude of the nature of diversity in Indian society whose features the Indian industry had inherited. Diversity is not an unmixed blessing for corporations and their management. Generally speaking, the weaknesses of societal diversity such as caste, for instance, are superimposed on its business and industrial organizations and exacerbated.

The marketplace and workforce in India are becoming more diverse every day. In fact, workplace diversity is considered a major challenge and opportunity for human resource management. It makes integration both difficult and easy depending on how diversity is viewed and used. The sources of diversity and its uses make a difference to what it means and how it impinges on organizational purpose and human behaviour at the workplace and beyond. Workplace diversity in India may have been partly inherited from centuries of customs and practices, partly imposed from colonial heritage and largely acquired through corporate omissions and commissions. They have implications for global competitiveness and for managing human resources/ industrial relations.

DIVERSITY AND INDIAN EMPLOYEES – ISSUES AND PREDICTIONS

Analysis of the 1991 census data reveals that the average family size among urban educated households is declining, with the extended joint Hindu family giving way, over the years, to the nuclear family consisting of wife, husband and immediate children. But the average number of dependants among these households is increasing due to migration of friends and relatives from rural households to urban areas in search of a livelihood. This is supposed to be increasing the interaction between rural and urban households in India and facilitating social change. Age mix diversity is found in organizations which has a long history. Such diversity is more glaring in such companies which: nearly stagnated for several years and suddenly experienced growth; are affected by mergers, acquisitions, etc.; and do not have a long-term human resource plan and did not have steady in-flows/out-flows of personnel. Such diversity can be handled well by long-term human resource plans, steady recruitment and measures to check erratic trends in employee turnover, etc.

The retirement age in the private sector starts from 55 years while that in the public sector starts from 60. In the past reduction in the age of retirement was considered at least partially useful in dealing with the problem of redundancy and unemployment.

In India the majority of the labour force is either illiterate or semi-literate. This is so even in urban areas and in industries which employ state-of-the-art technologies in old, established industries. In green field sites and in new, modern, microchip based firms the scenario is changing, but there is no readily available hard data to substantiate this. The proportion of skilled labour in the total labour force of the country being too small, there is a general dearth of skilled workers. Low literacy (52 per cent as per 1991 census) and skill obsolescence heightens the technological lag even in modern firms. The mismatch between acquired and required skills is evident by the rise in the educated unemployed on the one hand and the general dearth of skilled personnel on the other. India has, in effect, chosen to give more education at a higher price to a few who have already had more than average education, rather than work for sound education for all. The effect has been to have a trainable total workforce, and a flow of highly skilled people notoriously larger than the number of jobs available. A firm level survey of 99 randomly selected large and medium sized firms in India during 1991-92 also pointed to significant differences between private, public and multinational firms in respect of blue-collar and white-collar training.

Diversity in the social system of India could be either divisive or synergic, depending on how it is viewed and used. Caste, religion, region, language, sex, age and other demographic aspects are among the sources of diversity in any setting. In the Indian context, some of the sources of Indian tradition such as the nexus between caste and occupation are superimposed on the organizational structures. With the result we have four broad levels of hierarchy that broadly reflect the four levels of the caste system in Indian society i.e.

Class I (senior managers);

Class II (middle and junior managers);

Class III (clerical and skilled production and non-production workers, non-executive supervisors); and

Class IV (unskilled production workers, sweepers/janitors, etc.);

Earlier studies in the 1960s on the demographic profile of managers and workers in Indian organizations confirmed that while most of the Class I and II posts were the preserve of the so-called "upper castes", Class III comprised different castes in the Hindu social hierarchy. With the growth of the public sector, increases in literacy and the pursuit of affirmative action programmes for disadvantaged communities, the situation is now ameliorated to an extent, though differences based on traditional social classification are still dominant in civil and public services and large corporations, particularly in the private sector, which are not mandated to follow affirmative programmes.

Caste has always been a major source of diversity in Indian society and therefore in Indian organizations. There are about 3,000 castes in India and each one is a social unit in itself, its structures and strictures differing in each case. So strong is networking that even a change in religion does not alter an individual's position in the caste structure. The recent controversy over extension of caste-based reservations to underprivileged is one such manifestation.

In India there has been an endless debate on whether caste is synonymous with class because of the intricate nexus between economic backwardness and social backwardness.

AFFIRMATIVE ACTION IN INDIA

Indian managers, like their Western counterparts, underplay the importance of Indian social values (such as social relationships and interactions) and professed to value achievement, advancement, ability utilization, perusal development, and so on (including the peace of mind). It seems that Indians have acquired both indigenous and Western values. While the indigenous values are transmitted through primary socialization and sustained by social institution, the Western values are cultivated through management education and maintained by job demands in work organizations.

The Constitution of India allows affirmative action through reservations in education and employment. The Constitution also recognizes the principles of legal equality as a basic individual right. The directive principles of State Policy underscore the Constitution's commitment to social equality. The main challenge the Supreme Court has confronted concerned "reconciling formal legal equality as an individual right with substantive equality as a right attached to a group or classes of citizens". Regarding it some of the key features include:

- Articles 4-18 list the rights of equality under the Constitution of India which drew its inspiration fully from the Universal Human Rights Charter. Article 14 recognizes the fundamental right of equality before the law and equal protection of the law.

- Article 15 prohibits discrimination on grounds of religion, sex, caste or place of birth. However, it makes exceptions and special provisions for women and children as well as for the advancement of backward classes of citizens or for the scheduled castes and scheduled tribes.

- Article 16 guarantees equality of opportunity and non-discrimination in state employment subject to the following three exceptions:

  — Parliament can make prior residence in a State a requirement for appointment.

  — The law may require a particular religious affiliation from persons seeking appointment to an office in connection with the affairs of any religious or denominational institution.

  — The State may reserve posts in favour of any backward class of citizens not adequately represented in the service of the State.

- The Constitution, however, provides for adequate, not proportionate representation. What is adequate representation, can be, and has been, a matter of debate and dispute.

- Article 17 abolishes untouchability. A separate law was enacted prohibiting the practice. Violation of the law is made a recognized offence. Article 18 provides that no title, apart from a military or an academic distinction, shall be conferred by the State.

The Constitution of India provides for affirmative action through job reservations and these are based on caste plus socio-economic backwardness. Governments — both central and state — have also fixed quotas for women, SC, ST, OBC, disabled, ex-army personnel, and etc. in education and employment in the government sector. So far, such reservations are restricted to government run or government-aided institutions and not the private sector as such.

On 13 August 1990 the Central Government issued an office memorandum (OM) in pursuance of the recommendations made by the Mandal Commission. The progress made in affirmative action is quite significant and the effects of socio-cultural factors in performance planning and review are significant. In several large public enterprises it is not unusual to find different departments being dominated by people belonging to a particular region or caste. Even trade unions in certain metropolitan towns are beginning to be organized on caste lines. The employees' associations of scheduled castes and scheduled tribes and those for certain intermediate castes have greater solidarity among themselves than the traditional trade unions. The trade union movement in India was once dominated by the élite and caste Hindus. Over the years this has been changing and the social profile of the union leaders is broadly beginning to reflect the social composition of the workforce. Different political parties usually field candidates in general elections to the Parliament and the state assemblies' candidates belong to the dominant caste in the constituency concerned. Election analysts confirm caste as a major deciding factor influencing voters' choice.

The proposed legislation requires private organization employing more than 1000 staff to report annually to a government authority on their progress in implementing affirmative programs. Those employers who do not meet the requirements of that authority may be named in parliament. The Affirmative Action Agency has reported rates of compliance. India has set up, through separate Acts of Parliament, the following five commissions to deal with relevant issues of diversity:

- Human Rights Commission;

- National Commission on Women;

- Scheduled Caste and Scheduled Tribes Commission;

- Backward Classes Commission;

- Minorities Commission

Subsequently several state governments have also set up commissions for minorities, other backward communities and women with a view to recommend, formulate and implement measures.

There are a number of traditional and relatively contemporary sources of the dominant Indian values. The main traditional sources are the Hindu religion, the caste system of social stratification, and the agricultural mode of production which have jointly given rise to a asset of highly idealized moral values of religio-philosphical nature. They were tempted by centuries of event and experiences to appear as social values, the dominant among them being a preferences for (1) arranging ideas, persons, relationships, and all other conceivable tangible and intangible things hierarchically, (2) maintaining personalized relationships, (3) adopting a moralistic orientation to discharge duties and meet obligation to the family, friends and relatives, and (4) maintaining harmony and tolerance among in-group members.

The productive organization has also to devise a number of measures to facilitate the shifts in both — the subordinates and the leader — toward more effective practices. This can be done by building pressure at least in three ways:

- By providing new knowledge and experience of better ways of working and more egalitarians ways of relating with each other;

- By highlighting or expediting a crisis-like situation where the employee must change their ways of working and relating to others (e.g. team work) in order to survive; and

- By leadership efforts to reinterpret social values and task requirements in such a way that the employees perceives less of incongruence in what they at present believe and value and what they are expected to believe and value.

Market and strategically driven organizations should adopt SIHRM (strategic international human resource management techniques). The Japan Report highlights four dimensions, which are organizational goal attainment, proper use of personnel, organizational development, and cultivating technical skills in employees. Culture again appears in designing and implementing the proper use of personnel. It suggested integrating the universally tested techniques with the local cultural imperatives by moving carefully after examining all the contingent factors. Many organizations today are looking for more than just an effective employee. Cultural competency is the latest addition to the list of skills a professional needs to have. They are expected to adapt to the various competencies within the organization as firms look for talent that is exportable across the globe, ready to deliver at any geography. Pramoda Karkal, VP and MD, Johnson Controls says that 'Inclusion' is a state of accommodating differences and the most important element in creating a harmonious work environment. "Every organization is about people with diversity in gender, age, appearance, background, language, race, intelligence, religion, etc. It is an imperative task of HR and include or engage employees to achieve company objectives."

Cisco has an 'Inclusion and Diversity Council' programme, the objective of which is to promote a culture of inclusion. "We aspire for all our employees to understand and recognize that inclusion and diversity drive innovation. Cisco's vision is to attract and inspire the most talented people in the world and we can only do this by our ability to attracts, retain, develop and effectively lead a changing workforce. Diversity is, thus, a business imperative," adds Curtis. "At Cisco, they believe a culture of inclusion where diversity is valued and is essential for us to become a truly global company. Employees from different cultures, with different experiences, from different geographies, and with a variety of viewpoints, values, and styles of interaction combine their unique backgrounds to better understand the needs of our customers and to develop more innovative solutions," says Tracy Ann Curtis, Senior Manager, Diversity and Inclusion — Asia Pacific, Cisco.

Unisys also actively supports the concept of global diversity. "Diversity is not just a matter of race, gender, national origin or religions but about recognizing the differences that both separate and bind individuals and groups of all background. Global diversity allows us to harness innovation and market opportunity, and it promotes growth, change and prosperity," Saup Benny Augustine, Director, Human Resources, Unisys Global Services, India.

Chandan Chattaraj, Executive Director, HR, Xerox India Limited says that "having diversity at workplace is a blessing in disguise." According to him, ensuring diversity helps to improve culture, which becomes conducive to new ideas and more tolerance. "Diversity also helps to improve retention of employees. In fact, having a heterogeneous team reinforces a culture, which is accepting, open and fair. This helps in attracting more people as it reiterates the fact that the only criterion for promotion and recruitment is having potential and talent". Xerox also emphasizes on ethnic groups and the history of Xerox proves it. The company is taking affirmative action into consideration and do not have explicit policies of enforcing, but rather have guidelines and have worked on building a culture which ensures that people are treated fairly and there is no discrepancy. It also observed that women in general attached more importance to value diversity than men. Women were of the strong view that organizations must work towards hiring and retaining more women and ensuring development opportunities for women.

References

1. Adler, N.J, (1997), "International Dimensions of Organizational Behavior", Southwestern College Publishing, Cincinnati, OH.

2. Allport, G, (1954), "The Nature of Prejudice, Addison Wesley, Cambridge", MA.

3. Amanda Sinclair, (2000), "Women within diversity: risks and possibilities", Women in Management Review, Volume 15, pp. 237-246.

4. Amy McMillan-Capehart, (2005), "Configurational Framework for Diversity: Socialization and Culture", Personnel Review, Volume 34, pp. 488-503.

5. Anderson, J. C, Rungtusanatham, M, & Schroeder, R. G, (1994), "A theory of quality management underlying the Deming management method", Academy of Management Review, 19: 472-509.

6. Andrew Lindridge, (2005), "Religiosity and the Construction of a Cultural-consumption Identity", Journal of Consumer Marketing, Volume 22, pp. 142-151.

7. Anna-Maija Lamsa & Teppo Sintonen, (2006), "A narrative approach for organizational learning in a diverse organization", Journal of Workplace Learning, Volume 18, pp. 106-120.

8. Argyris, C, (1990), "Overcoming Organisational Defense Routines: Facilitating Organisational Learning", Allyn and Bacon, Boston, MA.

9. Ashkanasy, N, Gupta, V, Mayfield, M.F., Trevor-Roberts, E., (2004), "Future orientation", in House, R.J., Hanges, P.J., Javidan, M., Dorfman, P.W., Gupta, V. (Eds), Culture, Leadership and Organizations: The Globe Study of 62 Societies, Sage, Thousand Oaks, CA, pp.288.

10. Asma Bajwa & Jean Woodall, (2006), "Equal opportunity and diversity management meet downsizing a case study in the UK airline industry", Employee Relations, Vol.28 No. 1, pp. 46-61.

11. Atkinson, J W, (1964), 'Motivation', Van Nostrand, New York.

12. Bailyn, L, (2000), "Gender and diversity in organizations preconference presentation".

13. Bennett, M. J, (2005), "Intercultural Communication: A Current Perspective", (Ed) Harvey. P.C & Allard M.J.," Understanding and Managing Diversity, Readings, Cases, and Exercises, Prentice Hall of India Private Limited", New Delhi, p. 53.

14. Bergman, B, Krause, W, (1968), "Evaluating and Forecasting Progress in Racial Integration of Employment", Industrial and Labor Relations Review, Vol. 18, pp.399-409.

15. Berelson, B, & Steiner, G A, (1964), 'Human Behaviour: An Inventory of Scientific Findings', Harcourt, Brace and Wood, New York

16. Bhadury, J, Mighty, E.J, Damar, H, (2000), "Maximizing Workforce Diversity in Project Teams: a Network Flow Approach", Omega, Vol. 28, pp. 143-53.17.Bhargava, S, Herr, H., (1996), "How to Manage Gender Bias", Business Today, p. 157.

18. Bhatnagar, D., (1987), "A study of attitudes towards women managers in banks", Prajnan, Vol. 16, No.3, pp.263-81.

19. Blakar, R.M, (1985), "Towards a theory of communication in terms of preconditions: a conceptual framework and some empirical explorations", in Giles, H., St Clair, R.N. (Eds), Recent Advances is Language, Communication and Social Psychology, Lawrence Erlbaum Associates, London.

20. Bourges-Walegg, P and Scrivener, A.R, (1998), "Meaning; the Central Issue in Cross-Cultural HCI Design", Interacting with Computers Special Issue, 9, (3), p. 287-309.

21. Bowman, R.J, (2005), "Increasing Multicultural Understanding: Uncovering Stereotypes", (Ed) Harvey, P.C & Allard MJ. "

22. Brown, CD, Snedeker, C, Sykes, B. (Eds), (1997), "Conflict and Diversity", Hampton Press, Cresskill, NJ.

23. Brown, J. A. O, (1934), 'The Social Psychology of Industry', Pelican, London. Cartwright, D, & Zander, A, (1962), 'Group Dynamics: Research and Theory', Row Peterson, Evanston, Illinois.

24. Bryan, J.H, (1999), "The Diversity Imperative", Executive Excellence, pp.6.

25. Burke, R.J, McKeen, C.A, (1994), "Career development among managerial and professional women", in Davidson, M.J., Burke, R.J. (Eds), Women in Management: Current Research Issues, PCP, London.

26. Byars, L.L, Rue, L.W., (1994), "Human Resources Management", 4th ed., Irwin, Bun-Ridge, IL.

27. Campbell, D.J, (1988), "Task Complexity: A Review and Analysis", Academy of Management Review, Vol. 13, pp.40-52.

28. Carnevale, A.P, Stone, S. C, (1994), "Diversity: Beyond the Golden Rule", Training and Development, Vol. October pp.23-39.

29. Carol Agocs & Catherine Burr, (1996), "Employment Equity, Affirmative Action and Managing Diversity: Assessing the Differences, International Journal of Manpower", Volume 17 pp. 30-45.

30. Cascio, W.F, (1998), "Managing Human Resources - Productivity, Quality of Work Life, Profits", McGraw-Hill, Boston, MA.

31. Catalyst, (1999), "Women of Color in Corporate Management: Opportunities and Barriers, Catalyst", New York, NY.

32. Claire McCarty Kilian, Dawn Hukai & C. Elizabeth McCarty, (2005), "Building Diversity in the Pipeline to Corporate Leadership", Journal of Management Development, Volume 24, pp. 155-168.

33. Copeland, L, (1988), "Valuing Diversity, Part 2: Pioneers and Champions of Change", Personnel, July, pp.44-9.

34. Copeland, L, (1988),"Valuing diversity, Part 1: Making the Most of cultural Differences at the Workplace", Personnel, June, pp.52-60.35. Cornelius, N, (1999), "Human Resource Management: A Managerial Perspective", Thomson Business Press, Cornwall.

36. Corporate Leadership Council, (2001), "Women and Minorities in Leadership Development", Corporate Executive Board, Washington, DC.

37. Corporate Leadership Council, (2002), "Gender Statistics for North America, Europe and Australia", Corporate Executive Board, Washington, DC.

38. Corporate Leadership Council, (2002), "The Role of Leadership in Diversity Efforts", Corporate Executive Board, Washington, DC.

39. Corporate Leadership Council, (2002), "Strategies to Improve Diversity in Female and Minority Representation in Management", Corporate Executive Board, Washington, DC.

40. Cox, T, (1994), "A Comment on the Language of Diversity", Organization, Vol. 1 No.l, pp.51-8.

41. Cox, T. Jr, (1993), "Cultural Diversity in Organizations, Berrett-Koehler", San Francisco, CA.

42. Cox, T, Blake, S, (1991), "Managing Cultural Diversity: Implications for Organisational Competitiveness", Academy of Management Executive, Vol. 5 No.3, pp.45-56.

43. Cox, T, Lobel, S, McLeod, P. (1991), "Effects of Ethnic Group Cultural Differences on Cooperative and Competitive Behavior on A Group Task", Academy of Management Journal, Vol. 34 No.4, pp.827-47.

44. CSREES, (1997), "Diversity and Pluralism", Available at: www.reeusda.gov/diversity/workforce.htm.

45. D'Netto, B, (1994), "Information Processing and Reward Perception Accuracy", Doctoral Dissertation, State University of New York at Buffalo, Buffalo, NY.

46. Dass, P. and Parker, B, (1999), "Strategies for Managing Human Resource Diversity: from Resistance to Learning", Academy of Management Executive, pp 68-81.

47. Dayal, I, (1971), 'Confliction Intergroup Relations in New Concept in Management', Lalvani, Bombay.

48. De Janasz, S, Sullivan, S., Whiting, V., (2003), "Mentor Networks and Career Success: Lessons for Turbulent Times", The Academy of Management Executive, Vol. 17 No.4, pp.78-91.

49. DeEtta Jones, (1999), "The Definition of Diversity Two Views. A More Inclusive Definition", Journal of Library Administration, Volume: 27 Issue: 1/2.

50. Dessler, G, (1996), "Human Resource Management", 7th ed., Prentice-Hall, Englewood Cliffs, NJ.

51. Dixon-Kheir, C, (2001), "Aim for Quality Relationships to Keep Young, Diverse Workers", Society for Human Resources Management, Washington, DC, Managing Smart, 2Q.

52. Dogra D, (2005), "Management Education - Issues and Predilections", Excel Books, New Delhi, India, pp 11-27.53. Dogra D, (2006), 'Ishwar Dayal on Management - Behavioural Science Applications Ch: An Overview of Behaviour: The Group, Ane Books India, 73-80.

54. Dogra D, (2006), 'Ishwar Dayal on Management - Behavioural Science Applications, Ch: An Overview of Behaviour: The Individual, Ane Books India, 61-72.

55. Dogra D, (2006), 'Ishwar Dayal on Management - Education and Training', Ch: The Training of Executives: An Evaluation', Ane Books India, 83-87.

56. Dogra D., et. al, (2007), 'Family Managed, Multinationals and Public Sector Enterprises - The Strategic Choices for Global Competitiveness', Chapter on 'Job Satisfaction and Organizational Culture', Ane Books, India, pp 63-77

57. Dolan, K, (1996), "When Money isn't Enough", Forbes, pp.164-70.

58. Dominik Giiss, C, Nning In Brazil, India And German, "A Cross-Cultural Study, A Cultural Study, And A Model.Source:"http://web.cocc.edu/cagatucci/classes/engl390/.

59. Earnest Friday, & Shawnta S, Friday, (2003), "Managing Diversity Using A Strategic Planned Change Approach", Journal of Management Development, Volume 22, pp. 863-880.

60. Edeltraud Hanappi-Egger, (2006), "Gender and Diversity from A Management Perspective: Synonyms or Complements", Journal of Organisational Transformation and Social Change, Volume 3 Number 2.

61. Elisabeth M Wilson & Paul A lies, (1999), "Managing Diversity - An Employment and Service Delivery Challenge", International Journal of Public Sector Management, Volume 12, pp. 27-49.

62. Ellen Ernst Kossek, Karen S Markel & Patrick P. McHugh, (2003), "Increasing Diversity as an HRM Change Strategy", Journal of Organizational Change Management, Volume 16, pp. 328-352.

63. Ely, R, (1994), "The Effects of Organizational Demographics and Social Identity on Relationships among Professional Women", Administrative Science Quarterly, Vol. 39, pp.203-38.

64. "Equal Employment Opportunity Benchmarking Association™", EEOBA.

65. Farren, C, Nelson, B., (1999), "Retaining Diversity", Executive Excellence, pp.7.

66. Faundez, J, (1994), "Affirmative action: international perspectives", International Labour Organization, Geneva.

67. Fernandez, J.P, (1998), "Slaying the diversity dinosaur", Executive Excellence, pp.15.

68. Festinger, L, & Kelly, H, (1957), 'Changing Attitudes through Social Contact, Research Centre for Group Dynamics', University of Michigan, Ann Arobor.

69. Fiol, M., Huff, A.S, (1992), "Maps for Managers: Where Are We? Where Do We Go From Here?" Journal of Management Studies, Vol. 29 pp.267-85.

70. Fleury, M.T.L, (1999), "The Management of Culture Diversity: Lessons From Brazilian Companies", Industrial Management & Data Systems, Vol. 99 No.3, pp. 109-14.

71. Galinsky, E., Bond, J, (1998), "The 1998 Business Work-life Study: A Sourcebook, Families and Work Institute", New York, NY.

72. Gardenswartz & Rowe's, (2007), "Conferences and Public Programs".73. Gardenswartz, L., Rowe, A, (1998), "Why Diversity Matters", HR Focus, Vol. 75 No.7, pp.Sl-S3.

74. Geber, B, (1992), "Managing Diversity", Training, pp.23-30.

75. Gentile, M.C. (Eds), "Differences That Work: Organizational Excellence through Diversity", Harvard Business School Press, Boston, MA, 281-440-5044, July 3, 2007.

76. Gillian A. Maxwell, Sharon Blair & Marilyn McDougall, (2001), "Edging Towards Managing Diversity in Practice", Employee Relations, Volume 23, pp. 468-482.

77. Giscombe, K., Mattis, M, (2002), "Leveling the Playing Field for Women of Color in Corporate Management", Journal of Business Ethics, Vol. 37 No.l, pp.103.

78. Gloria E. Miller & Julie LA, Rowney, (1999), "Workplace Diversity Management in A Multicultural Society", Women in Management Review, Volume 14, pp. 307-315.

79. Goldberg, C.B, Zhang, L, (2006), "The Positive and Negative Effects of Racism and Sexism on Perceptions of Group Cohesiveness and Performance", Southern Management Association Proceedings, Clearwater Beach, FL.

80. Golnaz Sadri & Hoa Tran, (2002), "Managing Your Diverse Workforce Through Improved Communication", Journal of Management Development, Volume 21, pp. 227-237.

81. Haggerty, M., Johnson, C, (1995), "The Hidden Barriers of Occupational Segregation", Journal of Economic Issues, Vol. 29 No.l, pp.211-23.

82. Hamilton, C, (1992), "Affirmative Action and the Clash Of Experiential Realities", Annals of the American Academy of Political and Social Science, Vol. 523, pp. 10-18.

83. Harrison, D.A, Price, K.H., Bell, M.P., (1998), "Beyond Relational Demography: Time and the Effects of Surface and Deep-Level Diversity on Work Group Cohesion", Academy of Management Journal, Vol. 41, pp.96-107.

84. Harvey C.P. and M.J. Allard, (2005), "Understanding and Managing Diversity, Readings, Cases, and Exercises", Prentice Hall of India Private Limited, New Delhi.

85. Healy, G & F. Oikelome, (2007), "Equality and Diversity Actors: A Challenge to Traditional Industrial Relations", Academy of Management Journal, Volume 26 pp. 44-65.

86. Helen Juliette Muller, (1998), "American Indian Women Managers: Living in Two Worlds Journal of Management Inquiry", Vol. 7, No. 1, pp.4-28.

87. Hellriegel, D., Slocum, J.W, Woodman, R.W., (1995), "Organisational Behaviour", St Paul, MN.

88. Herzberg, F, Mausner, B, & Snydermaunn, B, (1960), 'The Motivation to Work', Wiley, New York.

89. Higgs, M., (1996), "Diversity management", Journal of Management Development, Vol. 6, No.3, pp. 134-44.

90. Hochschild, A, (1997), "The Time Bind: When Work Becomes Home and Home Becomes Work", Henry Holt & Company, New York, NY.

91. Hofstede, G, (1980), "Motivation, Leadership, and Organization: Do American Theories Apply Abroad", Organizational Dynamics, pp.42-63.92. Hofstede, G, (2001), "Culture's Consequences: "Comparing Values, Behaviours", Institutions and Organizations across Nations, Sage, Thousand Oaks", CA.

93. Hofstede, G, (2003), "Cultures and Organizations, Software of the Mind, Intercultural Cooperation and its Importance for Survival", McGraw-Hill, London.

94. Hofstede, G, Bond, M.H., (1988), "The Confucius Connection: From Cultural Roots to Economic Growth", Organizational Dynamics, Vol. 16, No.4, pp.4-21.

95. Hofstede, G, van Deusen, C, Mueller, C, Charles, T., (2002), "The Business Goals Network What Goals Do Business Leaders Pursue? A Study In Fifteen

Countries", Journal of International Business Studies, Vol. 33, No.4, pp.785-803.

96. Homans, G, (1950), 'The Human Group', Harcourt, Brace and Wood, New York.

97. Howard, Larry W, Foster, S. Thomas, (1999), "The Influence of Human Resource Practices on Empowerment and Employee Perceptions of Management Commitment to Quality", Journal of Quality Management", 10848568, Vol. 4, Issue 1.

98. http://www.thehindubusinessline.eom/manager/ 2006/07/31/stories/2006073100601300. htm.

99. lies, P, (1995), "Learning to work with difference", Personnel Review, Vol. 24, No.6, pp.44-60.

100. Ingrid Bonn, (2005), "Improving Strategic Thinking: A Multilevel Approach", Leadership & Organization Development Journal, Volume 26, pp. 336-354.

101. Jackson, B.W, LaFasto, F., Schultz, H.G., Kelly, D., (1992), "Diversity", Human Resource Management, Vol. 31, No.l and 2, pp.21-34.

102. Jackson, S.E, (1992), "Team Composition In Organizational Settings: Issues In Managing an Increasingly Diverse Workforce", in Worchel, S., Wood, W., Simpson, J.A. (Eds), Group Process and Productivity, Sage Publications, Newbury Park, CA, pp. 138-73.

103. Jackson, T, (2004), "Management and Change in

Africa: A Cross-cultural Perspective", Routledge, London.

104. Jain, H.C, Ratnam, C.S.V., (1994), "Affirmative Action In India: Reservations for Scheduled Castes and Scheduled Tribes in India", International Manpower Journal, Vol. 15,No.7.

105. Jain, H.C, Ratnam, C.S.V., (1996), "The Working of The Equal Remuneration Act in India", Monograph, McMaster University, Hamilton.

106. Jain, M, (1992), "The Changing Woman", India Today.

107. Jelinek, M., Litterer, J.A., (1994), "Towards A Cognitive Theory of Organizations", in Stubbart, C, Meindl, J.R., Porac, J.F. (Eds), Advances in Managerial Cognition and Organizational Information Processing, JAI Press, Greenwich, CT, Vol. 5, pp.3-41.

108. Jenkins, P and Wassener, B., (2004), "How Germany Keeps Women Off the Board", Financial Times.

109. Jenner, L, (1994), "Diversity Management: What Does It Mean?" HRFocus,Vol.71, No.l, pp.11.

110. Johnson, W.B, Packer, A.H., (1987), "Workforce 2000: Work and Workers for the Twenty-first Century", Hudson Institute, Indianapolis, IN.111. Johnston, W.B, (1991), "Global Workforce 2000: The New World Labour Market", Harvard Business Review, pp.115-27.

112. Julian Teicher and Katie Spearitt, (1996), "From Equal Employment Opportunity to Diversity Management", International Journal of Manpower, Vol.17, No.4/5, pp. 109-133.

113. Kandola, R. Fullerton, J, (1994), "Diversity: More Than Just an Empty Slogan", Personnel Management, Vol. 26 No.ll, pp.16-19.

114. Kahn, R L, & Boulding, E, (1964), 'Power and Conflict in Organisations', Basic Books, New York.

115. Kanter, R, (1977), "Men and Women of the Corporation", Basic Books, New York, NY.

116. Keough, K.A, Zibardo, P.G. Boyd, J.N, (1999), "Who's Smoking, Drinking, and Using Drugs? Time Perspective as A Predictor of Substance Use", Basic and Applied Social Psychology, Vol. 21 No.2, pp. 149-64.

117. Kikoski, J.F, Kikoski, C.K. (1996), "Reflexive Communication in the Culturally Diverse Workplace", Quorum Books, Westport, CT.

118. Koonce, R, (2001), "Redefining Diversity: It's Not Just The Right Thing To Do. It Also Makes Good Business Sense", Training & Development, Vol. 12 No. 12, pp.22-32.

119. Kossek, E.E, Lobel, S.A, (1996), "Introduction: Transforming Human Resource Systems to Manage Diversity", "Managing Diversity: Human Resource Strategies for Transforming the Workplace", Blackwell, Oxford, pp. 1-19.

120. Kundu, S.C, (2001), "Valuing Cultural Diversity: A Study of Employees' Reactions To Employer Efforts To Value Diversity In India", Proceedings of the 7th Asia-Pacific Management Conference - The Great Asia in 21st Century, University of Malaya, Kuala Lumpur, Malaysia and National Cheng Kung University, Tainan, Taiwan, ROC, Vol. II ,pp.635-46.

121. Langley, A, (1989), "In Search of Rationality: The Purposes Behind the Use of Formal Analysis in Organisations", Administrative Science Quarterly, pp.598-631.

122. Larkey, L.K, (1996), "Toward a Theory of Communicative Interactions In Culturally Diverse Workgroups", Academy of Management Review, Vol. 21 pp.463-91.

123. Lavaty, S, Kleiner, B.H, (2001), "Managing and Understanding the French Employee", Management Research News, Vol. 24 No.3/4, pp.45-8.

124. Leonard, D and Swap, W, (1999), "When Sparks Fly: Igniting Creativity In Groups. Harvard Business School Press", Cambridge, MA.

125. Leonard, J, (1983), "The Impact of Affirmative Action, US Department of Labor", Washington, DC.

126. Leonard, J, (1984), "Anti-Discrimination or Reverse Discrimination: The Impact of Changing Demographics, Title VII, And Affirmative Action on

Productivity", Journal of Human Resources, Vol. 19 No.2, pp.145-74.

127. Leonard, J, (1984), "Employment and Occupational Advance Under Affirmative Action", Review of Economics and Statistics, Vol. 66 No.3, pp.377-85.

128. Leonard, J, (1984), "The Impact of Affirmative Action on Employment", Journal of Labor Economics, Vol. 2 No.4, pp.439-63.129. Lewis, A., Fagenson, E, (1995), "Strategies for Developing Women Managers: How Well Do They Fulfill Their Objectives?" Journal of Management Development, Vol. 14 No.2, pp.39-53.

130. Linnehan, F., Konrad, A, (1999), "Diluting Diversity: Implications for Intergroup Inequality in Organizations", Journal of Management Inquiry, Vol. 8 No.4, pp.399-414.

131. Litterer, J A, (1973), 'The Analysis of Organisations', Wiley, New York.

132. Loden, M, Rosener, J.B, (1991), "Workforce America Managing Employee Diversity as a Vital Resource", Business One Irwin, Homewood, IL.

133. Maddock, S, Parkin, D, (1994), "Gender Cultures: How They Affect Men and Women at Work", in Davidson, M, Burke, R. (Eds), Women in Management: Current Research Issues, Paul Chapman Publishing Ltd., London, pp.29-40.

134. Magala, S, (2005), "Cross-cultural Competence", Routledge, London.

135. Mami Taniguchi, (2006), "Changes in Career Models Succeeding Where Others Fail To Try A Case Study of Diversity Management in The Japanese Retail Sector", Career Development International, Vo.22 No.3, pp.216-229.

136. Mankidy, J, (1995-1996), "Managing Human Resource Diversity: Challenges and Responses of the Indian Banking Industry", Prajnan, Vol. 24 No.4, pp.445-60.

137. Maria Humphries & Shayne Grice, (1995), "Equal Employment Opportunity and the Management of Diversity", Journal of Organizations Change Management, vol.8 No.5, pp. 17-32.

138. Maria Tereza Lema Fleury, (1999), "The Management of Culture Diversity: Lessons From Brazilian Companies", Industrial Management & Data Systems 99(3), pp. 109-114.

139. Marilyn McDougall, (Number 5/6 1996), "Equal Opportunities Versus Managing Diversity Another Challenge For Public Sector Management?" International Journal of Public Sector Management, Volume 9, pp. 62-72.

140. Marshall, J, (1984), "Women Managers: Travelers in a Male World", John Wiley, Chichester.

141. Mattis, M, (2001), "Advancing Women in Business Organizations: Key Leadership Roles and Behaviors of Senior Leaders And Middle Managers", Journal

of Management Development, Vol. 20 No.4, pp.371-88.

142. McClelland, D C, (1961), 'Achieving Society', The Free Press, New York.

143. McGuire, D, O'Donnell, D, Garavan, T.N, Saha, S.K, (2002), "The Cultural Boundedness of Theory and Practice In HBD?", Cross Cultural Management, Vol. 9 No.2, pp.25-44.

144. McNerney, D, (1994), "The Bottom Line Value of Diversity", HR Focus, Vol. May pp.22-3.

145. McNett, J, (2005), "Diversity In The Workplace: Ethics, Pragmatism, Or Some Of Both?", (Ed) Harvey, P.C & Allard M.J, "Understanding and Managing Diversity, Readings, Cases, and Exercises, Prentice Hall of India Private Limited, New Delhi, pp.242-248.

146. Mellahi, K. (2001), "Differences and Similarities In Future Managerial Values: A Five Cultures Comparative Study", Cross Cultural Management, Vol. 8 No.l, pp.45-58.147.Meyer, A, (2003), "The Experience of Human Diversity and the Search for Unity", Concepts of Mankind in the Late Enlightenment, Cromohs, 1-15.

148. Mills, A.J, Murgatroyd, J, (1994), "Organisational Rules: a Framework for Understanding Organisational Action", Houghton Mifflin, Boston, MA.

149. Moore, S. (1999), "Understanding and Managing Diversity Amongst Groups At Work: Key Issues for Organizational Training And Development", Journal of European Industrial Training, Vol. 23 No.4, 208-218.

150. Morrison, A, (1992), "The New Leaders: Guidelines on Leadership Diversity in America", Jossey Bass, San Francisco, CA.

151. Myloni, B, Harzing, A.W, and Mirza, (2003), "Human Resource Management in Greece Have the Colours of Culture Faded Away?", International Journal of Cross Cultural Management, Vol.4(l), pp. 59-76.

152. Nemetz, P.L, Christensen, S.L, (1996), "The Challenge of Cultural Diversity", Academy of Management Review", Vol. 21 No.2, pp.434-63.

153. Ng, W, Lee, S.F, Siores, E, (2003), "8C Plus 6C Management Model for Multi-National Corporation A Locally Compatible and Globally Fit Culture Model", Journal of Materials Processing Technology, Vol. 139 pp.44-50.

154. Nicolina Kamenou, (2006), "Ethnic Minority Women; A Lost Voice In HRM", Human resource management journal, Vol. 16 no.2.

155. Nina Jacob, (2005), "Cross-Cultural Investigations: Emerging Concepts", Journal of Organizational Change Management, Volume 18 pp. 514-528.

156. Noe, R.A, Hollenbeck, J.R, Gerhart, B, Wright, P.M, (1997), "Human Resource Management: Gaining a Competitive Advantage", Irwin, Chicago, IL,

157. Oya Aytemiz Seymen, (2006) "The Cultural Diversity Phenomenon in Organisations and Different Approaches For Effective Cultural Diversity Management: A Literary Review", Cross Cultural Management: An International Journal, Volume 13, pp. 296-315.

158. Parikh Indira J, (1998), "Paradigms of Gender Issues in Indian Organizations", IIMA Working Papers.

159. Parkin, F, (1979), "Marxism and Class Theory: A Bourgeois Critique", Tavistock Publications, London.

160. Patel, I, (1994), "Gender Differences in Employment Patterns of Doordarshan and All India Radio", Media Advocacy Group and Friedrich Ebert Stiftung, New Delhi..

161. Paula Ketter, (2006), "Newsflash, British Employers Prepare for Age Discrimination".

162. Porac, J.F, Thomas, H, Baden-Fuller, C, (1989), "Competitive Groups as Cognitive Communities: The Case Of Scottish Knitwear Manufacturers", Journal of Management Studies, Vol. 26 pp.397-416.

163. Porras, J.I, (1991), "Racism in A Research University: Some Observations and Comments", in Kossek, E.E., Zonia, S.C. (Eds), Journal of Organizational Behavior, Vol. 14 pp.61-81.

164. Pringle, J., Scowcroft, J, (1996), "Managing Diversity: Meaning and Practice in New Zealand Organizations", Asia Pacific Journal of Human Resources, Vol. 34 No.2, pp.28-43.165.Ragins, B, Cotton, J, (1996), "Jumping the Hurdles: Barriers to Mentoring for Women in Organizations", Leadership & Organization Development Journal, Vol. 17 No.3, pp.37-41.

166. Randlesome, C, (2002), "Diversity of Europe's Business Cultures Under Threat", Cross Cultural Management, Vol. 9 No.2, pp.65-76.

167. Rao, U, (2005), "Religion, Culture and Management in The New Millennium", (Ed) Harvey. P.C & Allard M.J, "Understanding and Managing Diversity, Readings, Cases, and Exercises", Prentice Hall of India Private Limited, New Delhi, pp. 179-183.

168. Reagans, R, Zuckerman, E, (2001), "Networks, Diversity and Productivity: The Social Capital of Corporate R&D Teams", Organization Science, Vol. 12 No.4, pp.502-17.

169. Reeves, C, & Hoy, F., (1993), "Employee Perceptions of Management Commitment and Customer Evaluations of Quality Service in Independent Firms", Journal of Small Business Management, 31: 52-59.

170. Reynolds, P.D, (1986), "Organizational Culture as Related to Industry, Position and Performance: A Preliminary Report", Journal of Management Studies, pp.333-45.

171. Rice, F, (1994), "How to Make Diversity Pay", Fortune, pp.45-9.

172. Riordan, C. M, & Gatewood, R. D, (1996), "Putting the 'E' (Employee) into Quality Efforts: A Process Model of Organizational Practices, Quality Principles, and Employee Reactions". In D. B. Fedor & S. Ghosh (Eds.), "Advances in the Management of Organizational Quality", Vol. 1: 299-335. Greenwich, CT: JAI Press.

173. Robbins, T. L, & Fredendall, L. D, (1995), "The Empowering Role of Self-Directed Work Teams in the Quality Focused Organization", Organization Development Journal, 13 (I):3-42.

174. Robinson, G & Dechant, K, (2005), "Building A Business Case for Diversity, (Ed) Harvey.P.C & Allard M.J, Understanding and Managing Diversity", Readings, Cases, and Exercises, Prentice Hall of India Private Limited , New Delhi, pp.235-238.

175. Roethlisberger, F J, (1959), 'Management and Morale', Harvard University Press, Bonson.

176. Ross, R, Schneider, R, (1992), "From Equality to Diversity - A Business Case for Equal Opportunities", Pitman Publishing, London.

177. Rumelhart, D.E, (1980), "Schemata: The Building-Blocks of Cognition", in Spiro, R.J, Bruce, B.C, Brewer, W.F, (Eds), "Theoretical Issues in Reading Comprehension', Lawrence Erlbaum Associates, Hillsdale, NJ, pp.33-58.

178. Rynes, S. L, & Trank, C. Q, (1996), "Moving Upstream in the Employment Relationship: Using Recruitment and Selection to Enhance Quality Outcomes", In D. B. Fedor & S, Ghosh, (Eds.), "Advances in the Management of Organizational Quality", Vol. 1: 79-140.Greenwich, CT: JAI Press.

179. S, Gayle Baugh, (2007), "The Southern Management Association Looks at Gender and Diversity", Equal Opportunities International, Volume 26 pp. 250-255.

180. Sally A, Martin Egge, (1999), "Creating an Environment of Mutual Respect Within the Multicultural Workplace Both at Home and Globally", Management Decision, Volume 37 pp. 24-28.181.Sarah Moore, (1999), "Understanding and Managing Diversity Among Groups at Work: Key Issues for Organisational Training and Development", Journal of European Industrial Training, Volume 23 pp. 208-218.

182. Schall, M.A, (1983), "A Communication-Rules Approach to Organizational Culture", Administrative Science Quarterly, Vol. 28 pp.557-81.

183. Schick Case, S, (1994), "Gender Differences in Communication and Behaviour in Organisations", in Davidson, M.J, Burke, R.J, (Eds), "Women in Management: Current Research Issues", PCP, London.

184. Sekaran, U, (1981), "A Study of Sex Role Differences in the Indian Banking Industry", Human Futures, Vol. 4 pp. 184-7.

185. Seyed-Mahmoud Aghazadeh, (2004), "Managing Workforce Diversity as an Essential Resource for Improving Organizational Performance", International Journal of Productivity and Performance Management, Volume 53 pp. 521-531.

186. Shellenbarger, S, (1995), "Women Indicated Satisfaction with Role of Big Breadwinner", The Wall Street Journal, pp.11.

187. Shelton, C, McKenna, M, Darling, J, (2002), "Leading in the Age of Paradox; Optimizing Behavioral Style, Job Fit and Cultural Cohesion", Leadership and Organizational Development Journal, Vol. 23 No.7, pp.372-9.

188. Shipper, F, & Manz, C. C, (1992). "Employee Self-Management Without Formally Designated Teams: An Alternative Road to Empowerment", Organizational Dynamics, 20 (3): 48-61.

189. Siddhartha Menon, (2005), "The Role of Diverse Institutional Agendas in the Importation of Convergence Policy into the Indian Communications Sector", Info, Volume 7, pp. 30-46.

190. Simmons, M, (1996), "New Leadership for Women and Men - Building an Inclusive Organization", Gower Publishing, Aldershot.

191. Singh, M, (2000), "Diversity Management in Educational Campuses", University News, Vol. 38No.40, pp.8-10.

192. Sinha, D & Tripathi, R. C, (1994), "Individualism in A Collectivist Culture. A Case Of Coexistence Of Opposites". In U. Kim, H. C. Triandis, C. Kagitcibasi, S. C. Choi & G. Yoon (Eds.), "Individualism and Collectivism. Theory, Method, and Applications" (pp. 123-136), Thousand Oaks, CA: Sage.

193. Sinha, D, (1996), "Culture as The Target And Culture as The Source: A Review Of Cross-Cultural Psychology In Asia", Psychology & Developing Societies, Vol. 8, No. 1,83-105.

194. Sinha, J.B.P, (1982), "The Hindu (Indian) Identity", Dynamische Psychiatrie, Vol. 15 pp. 148-60.

195. Sinha, J.B.P, (1984), "A Model of Effective Leadership Styles in India", International Studies of Management and Organization, Vol. 14 No.3, pp.86-98.

196. Smith, P.B, Peterson, M.F, Schwartz, S.H, (2002), "Cultural Values, Sources of Guidance and Their Relevance to Managerial Behaviour A 47 - Nation Study", Journal of Cross-Cultural Psychology, Vol. 33 No.2, pp. 188-208.

197. Source: http://www.answers.com/topic/affirmative-action198.   Sowell, T, (2005), "A World View of Cultural Diversity, (Ed) Harvey P.C & Allard M.J, Understanding and Managing Diversity", Readings,

Cases, and Exercises, Prentice Hall of India Private Limited , New Delhi, pp. 29-32.

199. Srinivas, M.N, (1952), "Religion and Society Among the Coorgs of South India", Clarendon Press, Oxford.

200. Stefan Groschl & Liz Doherty, (1999), "Diversity Management in Practice", International Journal of Contemporary Hospitality Management, Volume 11, pp. 262-268.

201. Steinberg, R, Shapiro, S, (1982), "Sex Differences in Personality Traits of Female and Male Master of Business Administration Students", Journal of Applied Psychology, Vol. 67No.3, pp.306-10.

202. Steven H. Appelbaum and Brenda M. Fewster, (2002), "Global Aviation Human Resource Management; Contemporary Recruitment and Selection and Diversity and Equal Opportunity Practices", Equal Opportunities International, Vol.21.

203. Stewart, A, (1986), "Performance appraisal", in Mumford A.(Ed.), Handbook of Management Development, 2nd ed, Gower Publishing Company, Aldershot.

204. Stringer, D, (1995), "The Role of Women in Workplace Diversity Consulting", Journal of Organizational Change Management, Vol. 8 No.l, pp.44-51.

205. Subhash C. Kundu, (2003), "Workforce Diversity Status: A Study of Employees Reactions", Industrial Management & Data Systems, Volume 103 pp. 215-226.

206. Suzuki, S, (1997), "Cultural Transmission in International Organizations: Impact of Interpersonal Communication Patterns in Intergroup Contexts", Human Communication Research, Vol. 24 No.I.

207. Tan, B.L.B, (2002), "Researching Managerial Values: A Cross-Cultural Comparison", Journal of Business Research, Vol. 55 pp.815-21.

208. Tayeb, M, (1997), "Islamic Revival in Asia And Human Resource Management", Employee Relations, Vol. 19 No.4, pp.352-64.

209. Taylor, W, Liss, S, (1992), "Affirmative Action in The 1990s: Staying the Course", Annals of the American Academy of Political and Social Science, Vol. 523 pp.30-7.

210. Thomas, D, (2001), "The Truth about Mentoring Minorities: Race Matters", Harvard Business Review, Vol. 79 No.4, pp.98-107.

211. Thomas, D.A & Ely, R. J, (2005), "Making Differences Matter: A New Paradigm for Managing Diversity", (Ed) Harvey. P.C & Allard M.J , "Understanding and Managing Diversity", Readings, Cases, and Exercises, Prentice Hall of India Private Limited, New Delhi, pp. 213-227.

212. Thomas, D.A, Ely, R, (1996), "Making Differences Matter: A New Paradigm for Managing Diversity", Harvard Business Review, pp.79-90.

213. Thomas, R. R. Jr, (1990), "From Affirmative Action to Affirming Diversity", Harvard Business Review.

214. Thony, W.P, Perrewe, P.I and Kacmar, R.M (1999), "Human Resource Management: A Strategic Approach", The Dryden Press, Fort Worth, TX.

215. Torres, C, Bruxelles, M, (1992), "Capitalizing on Global Diversity", HR Magazine, pp.30-3.216. Totta, J.M, Burke, R.J, (1995), "Integrating Diversity and Equality Into The Fabric of the Organisation", Women in Management Review, Vol. 10 No.7, pp.32-9.

217. Triandis, H, (1976), "The Future of Pluralism Revisited", Journal of Social Issues, Vol. 32 pp. 179-208.

218. Triandis, H, Hall, E, Ewen, R, (1965), "Member Heterogeneity and Dyadic Creativity", Human Relations, Vol. 18 pp.33-55.

219. Triandis, H.C (1995), "A Theoretical Framework For the Study of Diversity", in Chemers, M.M, Oskamp, S, Costanzo, M.A (Eds), "Diversity in Organizations: New Perspectives for a Changing Workplace", Sage, Thousand Oaks, CA, pp.11-36.

220. Trompenaars, F, Hampden-Turner, CM, (1998), "Riding the Waves of Culture: Understanding

Cultural Diversity in Global Business", 2nd ed., McGraw-Hill, New York, NY.

221. Tsui, A, Egan, T, O'Reilly, C. III, (1992), "Being Different: Relational Demography and Organizational Attachment", Administrative Science Quarterly, Vol. 37 pp.549-79.

222. Tsui, A, Gutek, B, (1999), "Demographic Differences in Organizations: Current Research & Future Directions", Lexington Books, New York, NY,

223. US Department of Labour, (1991), "A Report on the Glass Ceiling Initiative, US Department of Labour", Washington, DC.

224. Velma E. McCuiston, Barbara Ross Wooldridge & Chris K. Pierce, (2004) "Leading the Diverse Workforce, Profit, Prospects And Progress", Leadership & Organization Development Journal, Volume 25 pp. 73-92.

225. Venkata Ratnam, C.S & V, Chandra, (1996), "Sources of Diversity and the Challenge Before Human Resource Management in India", International Journal of Manpower, Volume 17 pp. 76-108.

226. Vince, R., Booth, C, (25-26), "Equalities and Organizational Design", Birmingham, paper presented at the International Research Symposium on Public Services Management at Aston University.

227. Wagner, W, Pfeffer, J, O'Reilly, C, (1984), "Organizational Demography and Turnover in Top-

Management Groups", Administrative Science Quarterly, Vol. 29 pp.74-92.

228. Waters, H, (1992), "Minority Leadership Problems", Journal of Education for Business, Vol. 68 No. 1, pp. 15-21.

229. Weick, K.E, (1979), "The Social Psychology of Organizing", Addison-Wesley, Reading, MA.

230. Wells, S, (2001), "A Female Executive is Hard to Find", HR Magazine, Vol. 46 No.6, pp.40-9.

231. Wentling. R.M, Palma-Rivas, N, (2000), "Current Status of Diversity Initiatives in Selected Multinational Corporations", Human Resource Development Quarterly, Vol. 11 No.I, pp.35-60.

232. Wharton, A, (1992), "The Social Construction of Gender and Race in Organizations: A Social Identity and Group Mobilization Perspective", in Tolbert, P.T, Bacharach, S.B (Eds), Research in the Sociology of Organizations, JAI Press, Greenwich, CT, Vol. 10 pp.55-84.

233. What is EEO? (2002) Fair Ways News letter No: 1320 5471234.White, R.D, (1999), "Managing the Diverse Organization: The Imperative for A New Multicultural Paradigm", http://www.pamy .com/ 99_4_4_white.htm (accessed November 14, 2003).

235. Wilie, R, (1961), 'The Self Concept", University of Nebraska Press, Nebraska.

236. Wilson, E, (1996), "Managing Diversity and HRD", in Stewart, J, McGoldrick, J. (Eds), HRD Perspectives, Strategies and Practice, Pitman, London,

237. Wilson, E, (1997), "A Women's Place? - A study of a National Health Service Trust", in Armistead, C, Kiely, J (Eds), "Effective Organizations: Looking to the Future", Cassell, London, pp.246-9..

238. Wilson, E, Doig, A, (1996), "The Shape of Ideology: Structure, Culture and Policy Delivery in the New Public Sector", Public Money and Management, Vol. 16 No.2, pp.53-61.

239. Wolf, W.C, Fligstein, N.D, (1979), "Sex and Authority in The Workplace: The Causes of Sexual Inequality", American Sociological Review, Vol. 44 pp.235-52

240. Yang Yang, (2005), "Developing Cultural Diversity Advantage: The Impact of Diversity Management Structures", Academy of Management Best Conference paper.

241. Zakaria, N, (2000), "The Effects of Cross-Cultural Training on the Acculturation Process of the Global Workforce", International Journal of Manpower, Vol. 21 No.6, pp.492-510.

Index